ROUTLEDGE LIBRARY EDITIONS:
THE GOLD STANDARD

Volume 2

THE DOWNFALL OF THE GOLD STANDARD

THE DOWNFALL OF THE GOLD STANDARD

GUSTAV CASSELL

Routledge
Taylor & Francis Group
LONDON AND NEW YORK

First published in 1936 by Frank Cass & Co. Ltd

This edition first published in 2018
by Routledge
2 Park Square, Milton Park, Abingdon, Oxon OX14 4RN

and by Routledge
711 Third Avenue, New York, NY 10017

Routledge is an imprint of the Taylor & Francis Group, an informa business

British Library Cataloguing in Publication Data
A catalogue record for this book is available from the British Library

ISBN: 978-1-138-56184-7 (Set)
ISBN: 978-1-351-24702-3 (Set) (ebk)
ISBN: 978-1-138-56899-0 (Volume 2) (hbk)
ISBN: 978-0-203-70445-5 (Volume 2) (ebk)

Publisher's Note
The publisher has gone to great lengths to ensure the quality of this reprint but points out that some imperfections in the original copies may be apparent.

Disclaimer
The publisher has made every effort to trace copyright holders and would welcome correspondence from those they have been unable to trace.

THE DOWNFALL
OF THE
GOLD STANDARD

GUSTAV CASSELL

FRANK CASS & CO. LTD.
1966

Published by Frank Cass & Co. Ltd.,
10 Woburn Walk, London W.C.1
by arrangement with Oxford University Press.

First Edition	1936
New Impression	1966

Printed in Holland by
N. V. Grafische Industrie Haarlem

PREFACE

TO form a broad conception of the true implications of what is going on day by day in one's own time is a difficult but most interesting task, to which intelligent observation will always be attracted. This task is never more fascinating and of more direct practical importance than when we are concerned with the unprecedented monetary revolutions that have taken place since the War. The ordinary routine-man is naturally inclined to judge these events from the point of view of the orthodox doctrine in which he has been brought up, and will then only be aware of occasional disturbances and of deviations from what he regards as a normal and natural course of development. In a wider perspective, however, it may be possible to perceive that the world's monetary system is undergoing a fundamental and definite transformation—inevitably accompanied by more or less violent disturbances. In fact, there is much evidence to confirm the view that we are passing through such a transformation, involving nothing less than the final dethronement of gold from its position as the basis of the world's monetary system.

In order rightly to understand the course of development, one must consult those documents that have most to tell us about what has actually happened and about the significant change of views that has gradually taken place. Want of first-hand knowledge in this respect has given rise to much confusion and faulty judgement. In the following pages, therefore, original documents have been quoted as fully as has been deemed necessary to supply the reader with the material that will enable him to form an independent opinion.

I have had opportunities of seeing much of the development from the inside, and I have had to state my views on different occasions, in conferences and committees, in lectures, books, and in the Press. The following exposition is largely based on this personal contact with the subject.

The view I express in the present book on the future of money has not been rashly or arbitrarily formed. I spent many years of hard work fighting for the restoration of an international gold standard. But when success seemed within reach, the forces of destruction again set in and swept away everything that had been accomplished. Careful examination of subsequent events has convinced me that a new attempt at restoration would be hopeless. But more than that: in the light of the experience that we now possess the shortcomings and defects of the gold standard appear to be so fundamental that the very idea of a return to such a system of money must be rejected as extremely hazardous; and we shall henceforth have to devote all our efforts to building up a new monetary system, entirely independent of gold.

The reader will find it natural, then, that I should feel the need for rendering account of my work in this field during the last twenty years and for proving that my efforts have been logically connected, although naturally varying with the steadily changing aspects of the monetary problem. To that extent this book has necessarily an autobiographical character.

The book is written not only for economists and bankers, but also for those of the general public who may be interested in following a narrative of the most perplexing events in the history of money and in getting glimpses of some of the most prominent actors in the great drama which is here described as 'the downfall of the gold standard'.

DJURSHOLM, G. C.
February 1936

CONTENTS

I. The Gold Standard in the Light of Pre-war Experience 1
II. The Post-war Reconstruction of the Gold Standard System 20
III. The Disruption of the New System . . 59
IV. Postponement of Monetary Reform . . 99
V. The End of the Gold Standard . . . 112
VI. The London Conference 135
VII. Silver 159
VIII. The Principal Monetary Systems after the London Conference 181
IX. The Illusion of a Return to Gold . . 212
Index 259

I

THE GOLD STANDARD IN THE LIGHT OF PRE-WAR EXPERIENCE

§ 1. *Nature and Defects of the Gold Standard*

THE international gold standard is by no means such an old and venerable institution as most people seem to believe. It is a monetary system constructed by Great Britain after the disorders of the Napoleonic Wars: it developed into an international gold standard after the Franco-German War in the beginning of the seventies. Gradually a series of countries joined this international monetary system, which became fairly universal when the United States, at the end of the century, after the great bimetallic struggle, had definitely established its monetary system on the basis of gold. This international system of money was maintained until the outbreak of the Great War in 1914, when it collapsed. Post-War monetary history is the record of strenuous efforts to restore an international gold-standard system, and of the final failure of those efforts.

Thus, in the perspective of the world's economic history, the international gold-standard system appears as a rather brief episode and can certainly not claim our veneration on the grounds of efficiency and stability documented through the ages. On the contrary, the short time it existed sufficed to expose the inherent weakness of the system. At first this weakness was not much noticed outside a narrow circle of experts; but the accumulated evidence of the normal functioning of the system and the subsequent catastrophic events were to demonstrate to the world at large the insuperable shortcomings of the gold standard as an international monetary system.

The theory of the international gold standard was very simple: if prices rose unduly in one country, that country's balance of trade would become unfavourable and the country would be exposed to a drain of gold with the consequence of a pressure on its price-level sufficient to restore the old price equilibrium. On the other hand, a country receiving gold imports on an unduly large scale would experience a rise of prices tending to counteract the import of gold. Thus the system would promote general stabilization, including both a suitable adjustment of the price-levels of the different countries to one another and a rational distribution of the world's monetary stock of gold. This valuable result would be attained by a machinery working automatically and in no need of being 'managed'. The automatic functioning of the gold standard was looked upon as its principal strength, the exclusion of all sorts of political influences upon the monetary system being held to be of primary importance.

However, in reality the system never—not even in the pre-War period of its existence—functioned in such a simple way. For the sake of security central banks had to keep larger gold reserves than those legally required and were therefore in a position both to export and to import gold without letting these gold movements necessarily influence the country's volume of means of payment or its internal price-level. The gold supply of a country exercised such an influence only via the policy of the central bank and its regulation of the market by means of its rate of discount and its open market operations. Thus the currency necessarily became a 'managed currency', whose value depended entirely on the policy of the central bank. True, the management was subject to the obligation that the currency should be redeemable in gold, but even if this condition were fulfilled—which was not always the case—it did not exclude temporary variations in the purchasing-power of the currency. In every business cycle such variations took place on a large scale and were more or less uniformly transmitted to all its members by the machinery of the gold-standard system.

The supposed automatic functioning of the international gold-standard system was further infringed by the movements of capital. A country normally exporting capital could compensate for a loss of gold simply by a reduction of its lending; and a country normally importing capital could compensate for a loss of gold by borrowing more. Thus it was possible to prevent gold imports or exports from having any influence on the price-level of the country and on the purchasing-power of its currency. Nor did the international gold-standard system guarantee a rational distribution of gold. Creditor countries were in a position to accumulate, if they chose to do so, disproportionate gold stocks without using them for any other purpose than for exercising political influence or merely for satisfying a national pride in the possession of gold. Debtor countries could provide gold reserves by increasing their foreign indebtedness. Generally, every member of the gold-standard system kept as large a reserve of gold as it thought desirable in view of existing legal requirements. The size of these reserves had very little to do with the balance of trade of the country. Nor did gold imports and exports have any distinct relation to changes in the balance of trade.

The fact that in spite of its shortcomings the pre-War gold standard did work fairly well can only be explained by the basic position that the pound sterling held in this system. Indeed, the pre-War gold-standard system may not inadequately be described as a sterling bloc held together by London's position as the world's financial clearing centre and by the service of the pound sterling as a generally recognized means for international payments. The strength of this sterling bloc lay in Britain's unbroken adherence to the principles of free trade and willingness to export capital, and in her abstention from using her position as a creditor country to accumulate an unnecessary amount of gold. Under such circumstances other countries, and particularly small ones, could be content with keeping their rates of exchange on London in the neighbourhood of par, and in reality they need not trouble themselves much about the working of the gold standard.

Thus the pre-War gold-standard system never attained those results which were constantly proclaimed, and generally believed, to represent its principal merits. It was never an automatic system, but had to be continually defended by means of a monetary policy directed towards its conservation. This monetary policy, however, did not lead to an ideal regulation of the supply of means of payment or of the general level of commodity prices. Rather, the endeavours to maintain the gold standard counteracted, in many respects, that true stability which should be the aim of rational monetary policy.

The pre-War gold standard was based on the tacit assumption that the value of gold itself could be regarded as stable and that therefore the maintenance of a fixed gold parity guaranteed the currency's satisfactory stability in purchasing-power. This assumption never corresponded to reality; even before the War variations in the value of gold in terms of commodities caused serious disturbances affecting the economy of the whole world.

These defects in the international gold-standard system became particularly patent when it had to face the tremendous strain of the post-War disturbances. We shall very much facilitate our examination of what actually happened in this period if we first devote some attention to the working of the gold standard before the War and to those fundamental defects in the system that already then began to manifest themselves. We shall find that these defects are of such essential importance that the gold-standard system must be said to suffer from an inherent and irreparable instability. This instability results partly from the instability of the value of gold itself, and partly from the insecurity of the redemption in gold of gold-standard currencies. In the two following paragraphs these different causes of instability will be more closely examined in the light of pre-War experience.

§ 2. *Instability of the Value of Gold*

The value of gold will be taken to mean here the purchasing-power of gold in relation to commodities. Variations in this value can be measured by some index of the general level of commodity prices, and before the War I made an analysis of the causes of such variations, particularly during the period 1850–1910.[1]

My main results are that during this period deviations of the actual gold supply from the normal gold supply are responsible for the greater part of the long-term variations in the value of gold, and that the rest of these variations are naturally explained as a result of particular and well-known variations in the monetary demand for gold. Thus there is no room for the many other explanations that have been offered, and the least that can be said of them is that nothing has been done to establish their validity.

The long-term variations in the value of gold during the period covered by my analysis cannot be regarded as negligible. In fact, Sauerbeck's index number of wholesale prices varies between a maximum of 111 for 1873 and a minimum of 61 for 1896. A commodity that shows such considerable variations in value in relation to other commodities can certainly not claim to represent an ideal standard of

[1] The first results were published in Swedish in *Ekonomisk Tidskrift*, 1904. A more elaborate analysis was incorporated in my *Theory of Social Economy* (original German edition 1918, English editions 1923 and 1932). A summary of my analysis is given in the *First Interim Report of the Gold Delegation of the League of Nations*, 1930. In my book, *On Quantitative Thinking in Economics* (hereafter referred to as *Quantitative Thinking*), Oxford, 1935, I have defended my method against some criticisms of it.

value. When this began to be acknowledged the question naturally arose: could the value of gold be expected to remain more stable in future than it had proved to be before the War? The answer depended on the prospective supply of gold and, in addition, on the possibility of so regulating the monetary demand for gold as to prevent this demand from causing considerable variations in the value of gold.

As to the first question, the analysis led to the following observations. Up to the War a general economic development in the world of Western civilization had been characterized by a fairly regular rate of progress of 3 per cent. annually. The average rate of growth of the world's *total* stock of gold very nearly corresponded to that figure. My calculations showed a rate of 2·8 per cent. per annum. More recent calculations referring to the *monetary* stock of gold come nearer to the figure of 3 per cent. *A priori* stability in the value of gold must be expected to require an annual growth of the gold stock corresponding to the general rate of progress of the world's economy. The objection has been brought against my calculations that the need for gold must have grown at a super-normal rate in a period when the gold standard was gradually extended until ultimately it included practically the whole of the civilized world. On the other hand, a certain saving in the use of gold is believed to have been attained by the steady growth of the use of cheques and clearings. With one exception mentioned below there is no reason for assuming that any of these factors grew so irregularly as to cause considerable variations in the value of gold; at any rate, for the period as a whole, they must have compensated one another, as the value of gold was at the end of the period practically the same as it had been at the beginning.

For the future the only possible forecast is that stability of the value of gold in an 'automatic' gold-standard system will require a growth of the world's stock of gold corresponding to the general rate of economic development. As the stock of gold grows the annual production required will grow proportionately. This observation raises the question whether in future we can expect the annual production of gold to increase at a rate of 3 per cent. a year, i.e. approximately to double every twenty-five years. Of course an economist cannot venture to prophesy about the future possibilities of gold production. He has to content himself with formulating the conditions under which gold production would be sufficient for maintaining a constant value of gold. As a matter of fact, the world's gold production was amply sufficient up to 1916, but after that year it fell more and more short of the requirement indicated. In the beginning of the twenties it amounted to about 2 per cent. of the accumulated stock of gold, i.e. it was only two-thirds of the normal figure. When, after the War, a restoration of the international gold-standard system was contemplated, an increasing scarcity in the supply of gold had to be taken into consideration as a most important factor in the problem.

Of course, it might be said that we do not know whether general economic progress will continue at a rate of 3 per cent. a year. If progress were to slow down, say to the rate of 2 per cent. a year, the necessary increase in gold production would be correspondingly reduced. But this way of putting the question is not very satisfactory. The aim of our monetary policy must be to create such conditions for the world's economy as will allow the widest possible room for progress. If a scanty supply of gold threatened to stand in the way of an economic progress otherwise possible, one could not recommend the restoration of the gold standard without indicating measures by which the scarcity of the supply of gold could be counterbalanced.

Thus the necessity arose of drawing up the outlines of a Gold Economizing Policy, aiming at a systematic reduction of the monetary demand for gold as compensation for an increasing scarcity in the supply of gold. How great was the part this programme came to play in the post-War endeavours towards monetary reconstruction will be seen from the following chapters of this book.

Even before the War, however, the demand for gold had shown some irregularities the effects of which on the value of gold could not be neglected. With regard to long-term variations in the value of gold, my investigations showed that the large accumulation of gold in the United States in preparation for the introduction of the gold standard so increased the scarcity of gold prevailing in the eighties as seriously to raise the value of gold and to depress the general level of commodity prices. I have estimated this effect at something like 7 per cent. This was enough to aggravate seriously the prolonged economic depression to which the world was exposed as a consequence of the gold scarcity, in the period from the Franco-German War to the opening up of the South African gold supply in the middle of the nineties. This was the first occasion on which the international gold-standard system was disturbed by monetary measures taken by the United States, but unfortunately it was not to be the last! A metallic standard always runs the risk of losing its stability if a Power with vast economic resources sets its mind on accumulating great stocks of that metal (as we shall see in Chapter VII). This danger has been demonstrated in the most striking way by the effects of the American silver purchases on the monetary system and the whole national economy of China. It is hardly possible to contemplate a return to any form of a gold standard unless sufficient safeguards can be found against such extraordinary disturbances of the gold market. In the post-War reconstruction period German reparations and the other War debts stand out as disturbances of the first order.

Turning our attention now to short-term fluctuations of the general level of commodity prices, we shall find that variations in the monetary demand for gold play an important and by no means a harmless part in these fluctuations. The elastic nature of the connexion between the supply of means of payment and the gold reserve enables central banks at the beginning of a boom period to continue extending credits with the result of a considerable rise of the general price-level. In such periods the existence of the gold standard has never proved to be a guarantee against undue fluctuations of the price-level. Before the War all boom periods were accompanied by a serious rise of the price-level.

When the boom broke down an extraordinary search arose for liquid assets, with the result that there was a general scramble for gold, a rise in its value, and a fall of the general price-level. An outside country would find itself exposed to a drain of gold and to the necessity of taking protective measures in the form of credit restrictions quite unwarranted by the country's internal economic position. In this way a crisis would be unnecessarily aggravated and would spread throughout the world. We see here that the very possibility of converting assets into gold entails serious consequences for monetary, as well as for general economic stability.

The extraordinary demand for gold with which we are here concerned may take the form of private hoarding. Usually, however, the central banks themselves are chiefly responsible for the injurious increase in the demand for gold inasmuch as they compete with one another in their endeavours to strengthen their reserves. In order to attract gold they raise their discount rates to a height that bears no relation to the internal situation, but is solely determined by the desire to keep the rates relatively higher than those of foreign central banks. This 'differential discount policy' was already before the War recognized to be a seriously disturbing element in the world's monetary system. International gold movements were to a large extent determined by this unsound competition for gold. The orthodox use of gold reserves for ironing out temporary deficits in the balance of trade fell into the background and often lost all importance in comparison with the gold movements caused by competition for gold and ultimately traceable to the artificial position given to gold in the world's monetary system.

The danger of a rush for gold in a time of economic difficulties was demonstrated most dramatically in the violent American crisis of 1907. The country was threatened by a complete break-down of its banking system and had to draw gold from Europe at any price. Thus the crisis was extended to this side of the Atlantic and caused severe disturbances that certainly could not be accounted for by the economic situation. This was a new lesson showing the dangers both of an inadequate monetary organization in the United States and of the possibility afforded by the gold-standard system of giving funds an artificial liquidity by turning them into gold.

Two more observations with regard to the effects of the gold standard should be noted here.

The artificial demand for gold that is fostered by the gold-standard system always has a tendency to strengthen protectionism. As long as it is possible to take gold as payment for exported goods people are inclined to look upon exports as desirable in themselves and are rather unwilling to accept foreign goods and services in payment for these exports. The revival of protectionism in the latter part of the nineteenth century and in the beginning of the twentieth is doubtless closely connected with the development of the international gold-standard system. We shall later on see what grave effects the post-War struggle for gold has had in this direction.

The economic development of the world has always depended very much upon the willingness of wealthy countries to invest their resources abroad. This willingness is, however, weakened if gold imports offer an opportunity to escape from the natural necessity of equalizing a favourable balance of payments by foreign investments. Certain signs of such an injurious effect of the gold standard were already apparent before the War, when some countries accumulated gold reserves to an unsound extent. After the War this effect was to grow enormously in its importance and in its destructive consequences.

§ 3. *Insecurity of Redemption*

The principal merit of the gold standard is commonly held to be that it offers the possessor of currency 'something tangible' into which he may convert his money. The underlying assumption is, then, that the currency of the central bank always remains redeemable in gold and that the individual is free to use the gold he acquires as he thinks expedient. But does the gold standard really give any such security? Was the individual, even under the relatively undisturbed conditions of the pre-War gold-standard system, in fact allowed freedom to convert his claims on the central bank into gold?

Nobody with any personal acquaintance of the functioning of the pre-War gold-standard system would answer this question with an unconditional 'Yes'. True, the convertibility of the British currency was not open to doubt. London always remained a free market for gold—a fact that emphasizes still more strongly the character of the pre-War gold standard as a sterling standard. But in other countries a free and unlimited redeemability was by no means guaranteed. Generally, the central banks eagerly watched their gold reserves and did not like any private interference with the gold movements, which they were inclined to regard as their own particular business. No doubt it was usually possible for the public to obtain small sums in gold coin for internal circulation. But if anybody wanted large sums of gold, particularly for export, he was most likely to be met with objections. A prominent Swedish banker once told me that if he had asked the Riksbank for any considerable sum of gold for export he would have been refused. This probably characterizes fairly well the atmosphere which prevailed in most central banks even at a time when redeemability was an officially proclaimed principle fortified by the strongest legal and constitutional guarantees.

The tendency to look upon the central bank as the only proper keeper of gold reserves seems gradually to have gained in strength during the short existence of the international gold-standard system. One sign of this tendency is the endeavour more and more to concentrate the national possession of gold in the reserve of the central bank. An effective method for this purpose was to issue small notes. In Sweden, where notes were issued in denominations of 5 and 10 kronen (one krone was about 10 per cent. more than one shilling), there never was any gold circulation. The German Reichsbank, which had not been entitled to issue notes of denominations less than 100 marks, was in 1906 allowed to issue 50- and 20-mark notes. The purpose of this measure was to enable the bank to strengthen its reserve by withdrawing gold coins from circulation. In fact, this strengthening of the gold reserve of the Reichsbank was generally spoken of as a great achievement of its then president, Dr. Havenstein.

Public interest in monetary matters became more and more centred in the gold reserve of the central bank. People were brought up to believe that this gold reserve could give the currency of the country a specific value which it did not already possess in virtue of its scarcity. The quotient of the gold 'cover' of the circulation was constantly published and brought into the centre of financial discussion. Thus the belief was fostered that the welfare of the nation depended upon the percentage at which the circulation was 'covered' by gold.

The legal regulation of the business of central banks likewise centred upon the gold reserve. The various but always quite arbitrary rules for establishing some arithmetical connexion between the gold reserve and the note circulation were discussed with a solemnity and an air of scientific importance that will seem ridiculous to later generations. Such rules had always the effect of fixing a certain minimum for the reserve. The consequence was that this minimum was withdrawn from every practical use. Central banks were therefore obliged normally to keep a reserve much above the legal minimum. The result of this system was that an essential part of the world's gold reserves became immobilized and that only so-called 'excess' reserves were at disposal for the purposes for which the reserves were held. In this immobilization of gold lay a great danger for the gold standard (as events during a subsequent period of gold scarcity were to demonstrate), in the form of an aggravation of the economic crisis and a general and very mischievous tendency towards deflation.

Gradually, the interest in the reserves was placed so much in the foreground that the maintenance and strengthening of reserves came to be regarded as the chief aim of monetary policy, far more important than the purpose for which reserves were held, viz. the redeemability of the currency. At the outbreak of the Great War the final proof was given of the dominating influence which this view had gained over monetary policy. In order to safeguard the reserves the redeemability of the currency was immediately suspended, even if some countries thought it advisable, by means of face-saving devices, to hide the disagreeable reality. This experience destroyed the idea that gold reserves were held to meet emergency demands. From that time it has been practically certain that, in any serious emergency, redeemability will be suspended and gold reserves will be locked up and will be of no use for safeguarding the currency. The motive will always be that the 'national interest' requires that 'the nation's gold' be concentrated in the vaults of the central bank. For this purpose even private gold possessions will be drawn into the central bank by more or less coercive methods.

These ideas, which already before the War had begun to dominate public opinion in all countries, are fundamentally opposed to the principle of the gold standard. If this monetary system has any definite meaning, its first principle must be the inalienable right of the individual to convert his currency into gold for free use. The corresponding obligation of the central bank must be upheld as a safeguard of the gold parity of the currency, equally important to the common interest of the nation as it is to the individual. If these principles weaken and gradually lose themselves in empty phrases, the decay of the international gold-standard system must be patent to any intelligent observer.

II

THE POST-WAR RECONSTRUCTION OF THE GOLD-STANDARD SYSTEM

§ 4. *General Conditions for a Return to Gold*

WHEN the Great War ended the world found itself involved in the most violent economic disturbances. It was a matter of extreme urgency to restore a certain minimum of stability and confidence. In no field was this more important than in that of monetary organization. However, governments and parliaments as well as central banks behaved as if they had no idea of this necessity. During the War pressing financial needs had tempted nations into the path of inflation, and after the War they simply went on, untroubled by any consciousness of the catastrophe to which such folly was bound to lead. Indeed, the inflation which took place after the War was in most countries much greater than that which had been directly connected with the War.

The fallacy of the official pronouncements on the nature of the rise in prices during the War was now demonstrated. In every country, even in Germany, it had been denied that the rise in prices had anything to do with a deterioration of the currency, and every effort had been made to make the public believe that the rise in prices was exclusively a result of war-time curtailment of the supply of commodities. I tried during the War to prove the wrongness of this view and to make approximate estimates of the actual progress of inflation in different countries. But people shut their eyes to such disagreeable truths, at any rate when the national currency was in question. The inflation of enemy currencies was recognized with greater acuteness.

The price that official ignorance and complacency had to pay for this refusal to recognize the truth was the post-War orgy of inflation. There were, however, some people who began to see the situation as it really was. The necessity of placing the world's economy again on a sound basis was perhaps most clearly perceived in the circles of private bankers and leading business men, and, of course, by some economists. These took the initiative in bringing about the first of the long series of international conferences which became such a prominent feature of the post-War period. This first conference was organized by the League of Nations and took place in Brussels in September–October 1920.

I had been invited to write for this Conference a memorandum 'On the World's Monetary Problems'.[1] This memorandum contained a chapter on

[1] Printed in Paper No. XIII of the Conference and later on reprinted under the title *The World's Monetary Problems. Two Memoranda*, London, Constable, 1921.

'The Gold Question', which began with the following paragraph:

'Whatever may be said, from a theoretical point of view, against gold as a standard of value, particularly with regard to the violent fall in the value of this metal which, as shown under (III), has taken place during recent years, it seems pretty sure that most countries look forward to the restoration of a gold standard and the resumption of gold payments as the real rescue from the hopeless muddle of the present paper-money system. We must reckon with this desire as a matter of fact, and we have, then, in the first place, to take account of its influence on the question of fixing the present fluctuating monetary standards at some definite values.'

In this chapter I further said:

'Though the enormous fall in the value of gold since the beginning of the war has certainly been a very injurious process, the inverse process of raising the value of gold would probably be still more disastrous. For the gold countries it would mean a prolonged process of deflation with all its pernicious effects on trade and enterprise and on the financial burdens of the State. For other countries it would seriously aggravate the restoration of a pre-war gold parity or the maintenance of a new established gold parity.

'It seems then, in the first instance, to be a common interest for the world *to prevent gold from rising again in value*. . . .

'To avoid this, it is necessary that all countries should abstain from measures for reintroducing an actual gold-circulation and content themselves with their present standard of gold holdings as basis for their paper-circulation.

Countries which are in a position to draw gold to themselves from the rest of the world should abstain from doing so. Thus the stabilization of the value of gold will clearly require, in the coming years, a close co-operation of all countries. Perhaps it will be possible to come to some international agreement in this matter. For instance, some measures in order to draw gold coins out of actual circulation, including eventually the stopping of all further coinage of gold, would be a natural object for such an agreement.'

As is seen from the above quotations I was by no means blind to the defects of the gold-standard system. But under the extremely disturbed conditions obtaining at the time I regarded a return to the gold standard as the only device likely to lead to a result in a sufficiently short time. However, I made this recommendation only on certain clearly specified conditions. A rise in the value of gold should be prevented, partly by abstaining from reintroducing gold coins, and partly by limiting the central banks' demand for gold reserves. Further, creditor countries should abstain from using their position to accumulate gold. This last point naturally referred in the first instance to the countries claiming reparations or War-debt payments. If the conditions thus specified were not fulfilled the restoration of an international gold-standard system must involve great dangers, for which my recommendation could in no way be responsible.

In the following year (1921) I presented a second memorandum to the Financial Committee of the League of Nations for their September meeting.[1] With regard to the bearing of reparation payments on the gold question I said in this memorandum (pp. 146–7):

'A disturbing element of a more technical nature, but of an immense practical importance, is the stipulation according to which the indemnity has to be paid in gold. The future value of gold is, as explained above, extremely uncertain, even the main factors determining it being beyond our control so long as no agreement has been reached between the leading countries with regard to their monetary demand for gold. The probabilities point, as we have seen, to an increasing scarcity of gold, with a consequent rise in the value of the metal. The stipulation of such huge payments in gold as the German indemnity represents cannot but materially affect the market, and will probably tend to strengthen still more the demand for gold in a world already insufficiently supplied. Thus it might easily happen that the enhanced value of gold made the burden of the indemnity much heavier than was originally contemplated, and in the end rendered it impossible to bear. At the same time, such a rise of the value of gold would make all other debts contracted in gold much heavier, and in many cases would completely undermine the solvency of debtors, public as well as private. In addition, all efforts and sacrifices for the restoration of a gold standard would probably prove futile, and the countries which had made

[1] Published in the book quoted on p. 21.

such attempts would find themselves thrown back again on a paper basis. Even if a country succeeded in keeping up the gold standard the confusion would hardly be diminished, for it would have to face a heavy fall in prices, and probably, as a result thereof, a serious depression in trade and production.

'It may be taken as certain that these grave consequences of the fixing of the indemnity in gold have not been taken sufficiently into consideration. There is, however, clearly no hope of a restoration of stability in the world's monetary system until some means has been found of removing this particularly disturbing factor.'

Speaking of the War debts generally I said (p. 129):

'It is easy enough to stipulate that such-and-such sums shall be paid in gold. But it is much more difficult to foresee what effect such stipulations, if actually enforced, will have on the gold market and on the value of gold. The mere existence of huge debts for which no regular machinery of payment has been provided makes the future of the value of gold extremely uncertain.'

I also pointed out the adverse effects which War-debt payments had in strengthening the protectionist movement (p. 150):

'The consequence has been a general growth of protectionism and, notwithstanding all that was said at the International Financial Conference at Brussels in favour of free trade and free intercourse between nations, the world is unmistakably moving in the opposite direction.'

I characterized these effects as 'most unfortunate and

injurious', and I also called attention to 'the immense difficulties of such a reorganization of the world's trade as must be required for effecting the payment' (p. 151).

Thus the general conditions for a restoration of the gold standard had been stated with sufficient clearness. In particular, the need for a progressive curtailment of the monetary demand for gold had been strongly emphasized. 'The only reasonable alternative to such a programme', I wrote in the second memorandum (p. 134), 'is the immediate and definite abandonment of the use of gold as a monetary standard.' The events of the succeeding fifteen years were to demonstrate with appalling harshness the dangers of disregarding these conditions. At the time when they were stated, however, men in political power thought themselves above such economic considerations. At any rate in regard to German reparation payments the worship of military power was still too strong to allow the recognition of any economic necessities to limit its freedom of action.

§ 5. *The Genoa Conference*

In 1922 an International Economic Conference met at Genoa. The principal motive for calling this Conference seems to have been the vain hope that it would be possible to reconstruct the economic life of Europe by means of an improved trade with Russia.

It should have been clear to everybody that it would take decades before revolutionized and ruined Russia could be of any help in promoting prosperity in other countries. The deliberations with Russia, which absorbed so much interest at the Genoa Conference and to which the statesmen at that Conference attached so much importance, naturally resulted in nothing. On the monetary question, however, the Genoa Conference presented resolutions which proved to be of great value and which actually served as the basis for the monetary reconstruction that took place in subsequent years. These resolutions were the result of the work of the Committee of Experts constituted at the Conference. The Report of this Committee was signed by Sir Basil Blackett (chairman), Professor Cassel, Dr. Havenstein, Dr. Vissering, M. Avenol, Sir Henry Strakosch, M. Dubois, Comm. Bianchini, and the Hon. R. H. Brand. The positive work of the Committee was mainly accomplished by the British members.

After having recommended a general balancing of budgets the Conference adopted two resolutions which it may be worth while to quote here.

'*Resolution* 8.

'The next step will be to determine and fix the gold value of the monetary unit. This step can only be taken in each country when the economic circumstances permit; for the country will then have to decide the question, whether to adopt the old gold parity or a new parity approximating to the exchange value of the monetary unit at the time.

'*Resolution* 9.

'These steps might by themselves suffice to establish a gold standard, but its successful maintenance would be materially promoted, not only by the proposed collaboration of central banks, but by an international Convention to be adopted at a suitable time. The purpose of the Convention would be to centralize and co-ordinate the demand for gold, and so to avoid those wide fluctuations in the purchasing power of gold, which might otherwise result from the simultaneous and competitive efforts of a number of countries to secure metallic reserves. The Convention should embody some means of economizing the use of gold by maintaining reserves in the form of foreign balances, such, for example, as the gold exchange standard, or an international clearing system.'

Further, in Resolution 11 it was proposed that the following more detailed programme should be considered at a meeting of the central banks:

'1. The Governments of the participating countries declare that the restoration of a gold standard is their ultimate object, and they agree to carry out, as rapidly as may be in their power, the following programme:

(*a*) In order to gain effective control of its own currency each Government must meet its annual expenditure without resorting to the creation of fiduciary money or credits for the purpose.

(*b*) The next step will be, as soon as the economic circumstances permit, to determine and fix the gold value of the monetary unit. This will not necessarily be at the former gold par.

(*c*) The gold value so fixed must then be made effective in a free exchange market.

(*d*) The maintenance of the currency at its gold value must be assured by the provision of an adequate reserve of approved assets, not necessarily gold.

'2. When progress permits, certain of the participating countries will establish a free market in gold and thus become gold centres.

'3. A participating country, in addition to any gold reserves held at home, may maintain in any other participating country reserves of approved assets in the form of bank balances, bills, short term securities or other suitable liquid resources.

'4. The ordinary practice of a participating country will be to buy and sell exchange on other participating countries within a prescribed fraction of parity, in exchange for its own currency on demand.

'5. The Convention will thus be based on a gold exchange standard. The condition of continuing membership will be the maintenance of the national currency unit at the prescribed value. Failure in this respect will entail suspension of the right to hold the reserve balances of other participating countries.

'6. Each country will be responsible for the necessary legislative and other measures required to maintain the international value of its currency at par, and will be left entirely free to devise and apply the means, whether through regulation of credit by central banks or otherwise.

'7. Credit will be regulated, not only with a view to maintaining the currencies at par with one another, but also with a view to preventing undue fluctuations in the purchasing power of gold. It is not contemplated, however, that the discretion of the central banks should be fettered by any definite rules framed for this purpose, but that their collaboration will have been assured in matters outside the province of the participating countries.'

The reader will find that these recommendations included two main points, viz. (1) the choice of suitable gold parities, and (2) a gold-economizing programme. The latter corresponded essentially to the recommendations referred to above (§ 4). But the proposal that gold coins should no more be used in circulation was excluded. In the Committee of Experts I had insisted upon such a recommendation, but as unanimity was required, it was dropped on account of opposition on the part of M. Dubois, a Swiss banker, at that time much trusted in international deliberations. Nevertheless, in the succeeding years this recommendation was recognized to be of the highest importance and played a principal part in the gold-economizing policy that was actually put into effect. The recommendation of keeping reserves in the form of balances in gold centres was also carried out, but later on this policy gave rise to much criticism.

It is perhaps not easy for a younger generation to

realize how much opposition was raised against the recommendations of the Conference with regard to the choice of new gold parities. Governments and central bank authorities had not yet clearly understood that substantial alterations in the values of the several currencies had taken place. They still entertained the idea that a restoration of pre-War gold parities was possible, and indeed was the only 'honest' solution of the monetary problem. For this reason the Committee of Experts had to hold out the choice of a suitable gold par as an act of particular merit. It may be of interest to quote here a paragraph on this subject from the preliminary observations with which the Committee of Experts presented their draft resolutions:

'The question of devaluation is one which must be decided upon by each country according to its view of its own special requirements. We think it important however to draw attention to some of the considerations which will necessarily weigh with any country in coming to a decision on this question. There is a prevalent belief that a return to pre-war gold parity is necessary or desirable for its own sake. There are undoubted advantages to be obtained by such a return, but we desire to point out that for countries where currency has fallen very far below the pre-war parity, a return to it must involve the social and economic dislocation attendant upon continuing readjustments of money-wages and prices, and a continual increase in the burden of internal debt. Regard being had to the very large debts which have been incurred since the Armistice by many of the countries concerned, we are inclined to think that a return to the old gold parity involves too heavy a strain upon production. We repeat that the decision must be left in each case to the country concerned, but we venture to suggest that a considerable service will be rendered both to its own internal economy and to the cause of European recovery by that country which, after reaching comparative stability in its currency at a point so far below the old parity as to make return to it a long and painful process, first decides boldly to set the example of securing immediate stability in terms of gold by fixing a new gold par at or near the figures at which comparative stability has been attained.'

In spite of this, as one would think, very convincing exposition, and in spite of the fact that the Conference unanimously adopted the resolutions, the representative of France rose to declare that his country would never devalue the franc: the French franc would again be put on its old gold basis and would once more become the leading currency on the European Continent. Representatives of the other Latin countries, thinking that they should not be inferior, made pronouncements to a similar effect. At that time a devaluation to a point slightly below half the pre-War gold parity would probably have sufficed for France. In 1928, after a long period of further inflation and monetary disorder, France had to accept a new gold par corresponding to about one-fifth of the pre-War parity. The other Latin currencies met with a similar fate. Nobody can wonder that, after these and a further series of equally discouraging experiences, economists have felt some difficulty in maintaining any particular veneration for the wisdom of the leaders of central banks or of government finance.

After the Genoa Conference I wrote an article[1] with the aim of clearing up ideas of what a return to the gold standard would actually mean and of the conditions required for such a step. In that article I specially emphasized the importance of choosing the new gold parity so that it should correspond as nearly as possible to the internal purchasing-power of the currency. I pointed out that the much-feared word 'devaluation' merely meant a public admission of a deterioration of the currency that had already taken place and a definite fixing of the monetary unit at its actual gold value. I added: 'If this value is very near the pre-war gold par, it will obviously be advisable to restore that par. But otherwise a new par should be fixed as soon as possible.' This recommendation was entirely in accordance with the Genoa resolutions.

I suggested that a general abolition of the use of gold in circulation was to be anticipated. To this

[1] *Quarterly Report of the Skandinaviska Kredit Aktiebolaget* (hereafter referred to as *Skand. Quarterly*), July 1922.

point I added an observation, which I should like to repeat here as it still has an important bearing on the gold-standard question:

'It may be asked what will then remain of the gold standard. Well, the principal thing, namely the maintenance of the currency at a fixed value in relation to gold. This signifies that for a certain amount in the currency one can always obtain a certain quantity of gold, and vice versa that for a certain quantity of gold it will always be possible to obtain a certain amount in the currency. These conditions, which are the essence of the gold standard, will always be fulfilled if the central bank is under obligation always to sell gold at a price *slightly above par and likewise always to buy gold at a price*[1] slightly below par. This obligation must obviously be supplemented by legal security for the free export and free import of gold. These regulations are sufficient to constitute a gold standard. It is, however, of fundamental importance that they should be so firmly established that the central bank will not be able to break through them in any way. Not till then will the commerce of the country attain that healthy development which can be based solely on a secure stability of the monetary system.'

§ 6. *Great Britain's Return to the Gold Standard*

The urgency of the stabilization of currencies on the basis of gold had been made clear enough at the Genoa Conference. Nevertheless, years were to go

[1] The words printed in italics appeared in the Swedish text but were accidentally omitted in the English translation.

by before any definite action was taken—to the great detriment of the world economy.

The complete collapse of the German currency towards the end of 1923 made the creation of an entirely new German currency necessary. In this extraordinarily difficult task the Minister of Finance and later Chancellor of the Reich, Dr. Luther, assisted by Dr. Schacht, rendered singularly good service. With the introduction of the Dawes Plan, and by aid of the so-called Dawes Loan, the new currency was given a gold par equal to that of the pre-War mark (October 1924). This important achievement naturally strengthened the desire of other countries to put their currencies on a gold basis.

Sweden was the first country in Europe to restore its pre-War gold standard. As the Swedish currency had been seriously inflated in the boom period that ended in 1920 the country had to go through a very trying process of deflation, with tremendous loss to undertakings which had relied upon some stability in the value of the country's currency. The deflation also involved considerable reductions in nominal wages, which the boom had raised to an abnormal height. However, this process of deflation was already nearly complete in 1922, and from that time on the Swedish currency was quoted very nearly at its old par with the dollar. Thus the restoration of the gold standard in April 1924 was well prepared. By means of a radical rationalization and a general reduction of costs, Swedish industry had adapted itself to the relatively high exchange value of the krone fixed by this reform. In the following years and up to the world crisis in 1929 Sweden had no difficulty in maintaining her gold standard. These experiences are of great interest as parallel to the much-debated difficulties and misfortunes that attended Great Britain's return to the gold standard in 1925.

When the Genoa Conference recommended that certain countries should establish a free market in gold and thus become gold centres it obviously had in mind that Great Britain should be the principal gold centre by the side of the United States, and it was taken for granted that the British currency would be restored to the old gold parity. The ground for this view was not only that the pound sterling was comparatively near to its old gold parity, but also that the restoration of the pound to that parity was of essential importance, having regard to the nature of the pound as a currency of wide international use and to London's position as the monetary centre of the world. Nevertheless, Great Britain hesitated to take a step implying a deflation by which the internal purchasing-power of the pound would be brought up to parity with that of the dollar. When finally, in April 1925, Mr. Churchill, as Chancellor of the Exchequer, restored the pound sterling to its old gold parity, the necessary deflation was not yet completed, and a somewhat uncomfortable process of adjustment was forced upon the country. Strong opposition was raised to the measure, particularly on the part of British industry. This opposition was very much strengthened by the support of Mr. Keynes, who led a vigorous campaign against a return to the gold standard. No doubt the opposition stressed the difficulties of the adjustment required, sometimes with exaggeration.

For my own part I quite realized that there was some friction to overcome, but I estimated that the necessary lowering of the British price-level at the beginning of the year hardly amounted to much more than 6 per cent.; and that the inconvenience of such a moderate deflation was a price well worth paying for the immense advantage of restoring the pound sterling to its old central position in the world's monetary system. In consequence of the restoration of the gold standard the British price-level was actually forced down, so that already in June practical equality with that of the United States was attained. These calculations were based on wholesale commodity price-indices, and the objection could be made that wages and other elements of cost were at a higher level in Great Britain than in America, and, moreover, were so rigid that an adjustment would encounter great difficulties. These arguments were, however, overstated and the conclusions drawn from them went too far. In this respect the experience of Sweden was instructive. Sweden had succeeded in carrying through the adjustment necessary for attaining the dollar parity. And as inflation in Sweden had gone considerably farther than in Great Britain, Sweden had had serious difficulties to overcome. The British price-level, according to the index of the Board of Trade, reached an average for 1920 of 307. The corresponding official index for Sweden showed an average of 359. In 1923 the Swedish price-level had been pressed down to 163 as average for the year, whereas the British price-level had already attained as low a figure as 159. The corresponding American price-level was then 154 and an adjustment of the British price-level to the American would at that time have been easy. Unfortunately, the British price-level rose after the middle of 1923 and reached a new maximum of 171 in January 1925. At that time the Swedish index was only 169, and the American 160. In July 1925 a practical equality of the price-levels had been attained, the Swedish index standing at 161, the British at 158, and the American at 160.

These figures certainly do not give the impression that Great Britain had greater difficulties than Sweden in carrying through the necessary adjustment of her price-level. As for the rigidity of British wages, it must be remembered that the Trade Union movement in Sweden is at least as strong as that in Great Britain.

On the second reading of the Bill for the Restoration of the Gold Standard Mr. Snowden (now Viscount Snowden), on behalf of the Labour Party, moved an amendment in these words:

'This House cannot at present assent to the Second Reading of a Bill which by providing for a return to the Gold Standard with undue precipitancy may aggravate the existing grave conditions of employment and trade depreciation.'

In moving this amendment he explained that he had always been in favour of a return to the gold standard, but did not believe that the present was the time when such a step should be taken, having in view the grave and serious consequences that might ensue. There was a disparity between Great Britain and the United States in the prices converted to a gold basis, the United States' price-level being probably 5 to 10 per cent. lower than the price-level in Great Britain. The Labour Party were of the opinion that a return to the gold standard ought to have been delayed until the prices on a gold basis had been brought to the same level in the two countries.[1]

In the ensuing debate Mr. Churchill answered that the Labour Party had previously expressed themselves in favour of a return to a gold standard at the earliest opportunity. The same view had been taken

[1] Viscount Snowden's *Autobiography*, p. 722 (London, 1934).

by Mr. Snowden himself. The explanation of the change of view, Mr. Churchill suggested, was that the Opposition wanted, if the results were unsatisfactory, to be able to say, 'I told you so.' This is actually the attitude taken by Viscount Snowden in his autobiography, where he writes: 'Our Amendment was opposed in the House of Commons by financial authorities, who later came round to our point of view and attributed the causes of the severe trade depression which followed to this precipitate step.'

In my opinion Mr. Churchill was quite right in deciding to return to the gold standard at that particular time. It was very important, and indeed urgent, that the pound sterling should again be based on gold and even be brought back to its old gold parity. The relatively small sacrifices involved in that step were much more than counterbalanced by the restoration of international confidence and by the stimulus given to international trade through the replacement of the pound sterling in its old position as the principal currency of the world's trade. If Great Britain wanted to restore the gold standard, this step, which for years had been generally anticipated, could not be postponed any longer without grave inconvenience.

It was reasonable at that time to suppose that international co-operation would be able, at least for the near future, to give to the value of gold a fair degree of stability. The gold-economizing policy, which had been recommended by the Genoa Conference and strengthened by the subsequent exclusion of gold coins from circulation, and which formed part of Mr. Churchill's reform, could be assumed to be effective enough to prevent a disastrous rise in the value of gold and the consequent necessity for a further deflation of gold currencies. The curious fear that Europe might be exposed to a flood of American gold, should America choose to part with her gold surplus, could safely be rejected as theoretical. As Mr. Churchill pointed out in his answer to Mr. Snowden's remarks on this danger, Great Britain was always in a position to meet such a contingency by sending back the gold in payment of her War debt to the United States.

The clause by which Mr. Churchill abolished the use of gold coins in circulation, and for which he gave the reason that such a use of gold 'would be an unwarrantable extravagance which our present financial stringency by no means allows us to indulge in',[1] was in fact a measure that will stand for all time as a milestone in the world's monetary history. We can now trace this history back to Babylonian times—some 2,000 years B.C. In it the use of coins occupies the time from the first mintings in Asia Minor and Greece

[1] *Parliamentary Debates*, vol. clxxxiii, col. 55.

some six or seven centuries B.C. up to Mr. Winston Churchill's Gold Standard Bill in 1925. For the world at large the circulation of gold as standard coin is a thing of the past, and it is at last beginning to be understood that the essence of money is something more than a mere piece of metal.

§ 7. *The Consequences of Great Britain's Return to Gold*

The British Dominions joined the mother country in the restoration of the gold standard. Switzerland and Holland with her colonies also restored the old gold parity of their currencies. These countries, together with the countries already on a gold basis, formed an international gold-standard system which soon came to embrace the greater part of the commercial world. An important step in this direction was taken when the Indian currency was placed on a gold basis. The idea of putting gold coins into circulation, which was popular in India, was properly rejected as being contrary to the gold-economizing policy. In this case, an excellent example was set of true international co-operation in monetary management.[1]

Undoubtedly, this world-wide monetary reconstruction contributed greatly to the restoration of

[1] Royal Commission of Indian Currency and Finance, *Report*, 1926, p. 15; and my *Statement of Evidence* (vol. iii, p. 594).

stability and confidence and served as an effective stimulus to the renascence of international trade.

To attain these ends had been the chief motive in Great Britain's return to the gold standard. That country had a paramount interest in the development of the world's trade, shipping, and finance. It seems natural and right, therefore, that public attention should be drawn in the first place to these results and not be allowed to dwell exclusively on the monetary friction connected with the reform of 1925. According to the statistics of the League of Nations[1] the world's primary production rose from an index number of 95 for 1925 to 106 for 1929 (average 1925–9 = 100). Agricultural production rose from 97 to 103 and non-agricultural production from 90 to 114. Thus, during the four-year period from 1925 to 1929, agricultural production rose, in round figures, by 1·5 per cent., and non-agricultural production by 6 per cent. a year. During the same time the volume of international trade rose from 91 to 110, i.e. by nearly 5 per cent. a year. These figures show that the depression had been surmounted and that a rather more than normal rate of progress had been attained. It is not too much to say that the restoration of the gold standard in 1925 was an essential factor in this favourable development.

To a certain extent Great Britain shared this

[1] *World Production and Prices*, Geneva 1935.

progress. In spite of the extraordinary labour disputes in 1926 the number of employed persons in the six years from the middle of 1923 to the middle of 1929 rose by roughly 10 per cent., which must be considered a very good figure.[1] True, the value of British exports, as expressed in pound sterling, fell off slightly from the maximum attained in 1924; but, reduced to the 1924 price-level, it actually rose. The serious troubles of the coal industry originated in profound changes in the coal market and cannot reasonably be ascribed to Great Britain's return to gold. To a certain degree the same holds good with regard to the cotton industry. It would have experienced a depression even if the world's monetary system had been in perfect order.

However, the continuous fall of the British price-level, which set in after 1925, caused difficulties which became more and more apparent and which, if the movement were to continue, must prove intolerable. It is wrong to explain all Great Britain's later troubles by the moderate deflation that was required at the time of Mr. Churchill's reform to bring the purchasing-power of the pound up to a level with that of the dollar. In October 1924 the price-index of the Board of Trade was 170; in October 1925 it had been reduced to 155. This deflation of not quite 9 per

[1] *Bank of England Statistical Summary*, September 1935, p. 113, diagram.

cent. was doubtless something that could be managed without grave or lasting consequences for the economic life of the country. But the deflation which took place later in the United States, and which forced Great Britain to lower its price-level to 99 in September 1931 (i.e. to cut it down by a further 36 per cent.), brought British economy into extreme, and eventually unbearable, straits. Had gold retained a constant value, as it was naturally supposed in 1925 that it would, the economy of the country could easily have adapted itself to the new external value of the pound. What made the whole situation intolerable was the tremendous *rise in the value of gold* which took place *after* 1925 and which, in September 1931, reached a figure somewhere between 50 and 60 per cent. The fundamental conditions for maintaining the value of gold at a reasonable stability had not been fulfilled, and for this reason the international gold-standard system proved impracticable. The failure was due to inherent faults in the gold standard itself, not to a premature adoption of it. This lesson should have a wide bearing on the present discussion of monetary reconstruction.

Those people in England who opposed a return to the gold standard in 1925 were naturally inclined to see in the subsequent bitter experiences a confirmation of their criticism, and did everything in their power to propagate this view. To the great prejudice of sound judgement and of the public's understanding of the true nature of the monetary problem this view gradually came to prevail. It became quite a common creed that England's economic and social troubles after 1925 were due to the 'premature' step of restoring the pound to its old gold par at a time when its internal purchasing-power was still some few per cent. too low. This dogma, which is constantly and thoughtlessly repeated, blocks the way to any deeper discussion of the monetary problem. The consequences are not only that the step taken in 1925 has been unfairly judged, but also that the real causes of the later economic difficulties and of the ultimate collapse of the British gold standard have never been brought into full daylight. For this reason the intrinsic faults in the international gold-standard system and the hopelessness of all endeavours once again to build up such a system are, up to the present time, very imperfectly understood.

§ 8. *France joins the Gold-standard System*

After the Genoa Conference the French franc deteriorated more and more. Finding itself in continual financial embarrassment the State resorted to an inflation of the currency. The note circulation of the Bank of France rose from a figure of 36·4 (in thousand million francs) at the end of 1922 to 56·0 in July 1926. The general price-level as measured by annual average index figures (*Statistique Générale*) was brought up from 327 in 1922 to 703 in 1926. The monthly index reached a maximum of 837 in July 1926. This internal deterioration of the franc was reflected in its foreign exchange value. The annual average of the New York quotation of the franc fell from 8·20 in 1922 to 3·24 cents in 1926. In July 1926 the very low minimum of 2·06 was reached.[1] After this fearful collapse M. Poincaré took the lead in the Government and soon succeeded in practically stabilizing the franc at a rate of 3·92 cents.

In June 1928 France returned to the gold standard at this par of 3·92 cents as against the pre-War par of 19·30. Thus the gold par of the French currency was reduced to a figure only slightly more than 20 per cent. of the pre-War value. This radical cut in the gold value of the franc was naturally received with great dissatisfaction by a nation of savers, and the Government had to hold out the prospect of a later improvement in the gold value of the franc.

It would seem as if the international gold-standard system ought to have been strengthened by the entrance of France into the system. The actual result was just the contrary. From that time on the gold standard began to show its inherent faults, and gradually a situation developed that could not but end in a complete break-down.

[1] *Federal Reserve Bulletin.*

In order to have a margin of safety the French authorities had chosen a comparatively low gold value for the franc. If we compare the French wholesale price-index for June 1928, 626, with the English one, as calculated by the Board of Trade, 143, we find that the pre-War par value of the pound, fr. 25·225, ought to have been replaced by a new par slightly above fr. 110 for the pound. The gold par actually fixed corresponded to a sterling par of 124·21. According to this calculation the new French franc was undervalued by about 11 per cent. Of course, after such extreme variations in the purchasing-power of currencies and such changes in the conditions of international trade it is impossible to calculate an exact figure for the true purchasing-power parity between two currencies. But that the revaluation of the franc in 1928 involved a considerable undervaluation is beyond doubt, and was even at the time generally recognized. This undervaluation, which had been still greater in the two previous years, gave France at least temporary advantages for her export trade and at the same time served as a protection for her home industry.

These conditions naturally caused some uneasiness in countries that were most exposed to French competition and in foreign export industries dependent on the French market. In England, the complaints about the burden which the nation had assumed by returning to the old gold par gained considerably in strength by the undervaluation of the French franc. Thus the demand for protection increased, and a new and strong weapon was put into the hands of the advocates of a tariff policy.

With the return of confidence in France and in the French currency, French capital streamed back to France, to a great extent in the form of gold imports. France's receipts on account of German reparations and her favourable balance of payments, combined with her aversion to new foreign investments, went to swell and perpetuate this stream. These French gold imports caused a drain of gold from a great part of the outside world. Thus the troublesome scarcity of gold that resulted from insufficient production of the metal was aggravated and a general process of deflation was forced upon all gold-standard countries, with the consequence of increasing difficulties for the world economy.

The question how far the responsibility for these French gold imports and their pernicious effects must be laid on the French authorities has been very much discussed. It has been contended that, when once the French franc had been stabilized and the French budget brought into equilibrium, gold poured automatically into France and that neither the Government nor the Bank of France did anything to encourage this movement. On the other hand, it has been pointed out that France by her tariff policy made great efforts to prevent payments to France being made in commodities; and that at the same time a natural export of capital was hampered by legal and administrative restrictions and by heavy taxation. The inadequate organization of the Paris money market was also an obstacle to the free outflow of capital. It is not necessary here to prolong this controversy. After all, the French nation was quite pleased and proud to possess such a tremendous gold reserve, and saw in it—as they were systematically brought up to do—an indispensable condition for confidence in the franc and the basis of the nation's economic and political strength.

From the point of view of the world's monetary organization what matters is the fact that a great creditor country during a series of years attracted such large quantities of gold that the international gold-standard system was thereby seriously threatened and a most harmful process of deflation imposed upon the world. It should also be noted that the gold imports into France served to swell the hoarding of gold. The hoarding of French banknotes which actually took place and which, according to the official view, necessitated the keeping of a corresponding gold reserve, was in effect equivalent to a hoarding of gold. Here we have an outstanding case in which a general desire for liquidity has caused an extraordinary demand for gold resulting in a very detrimental increase in the value of gold. This experience proves that the value of gold has no intrinsic stability but may at any time be subject to changes of the most arbitrary nature.

§ 9. *Elements of Instability in the New Monetary System*

Viewed in the light of subsequent events, the post-War endeavours to reconstruct an international gold-standard system had been crowned with great success. True, the reconstruction had been unduly delayed, principally because some countries were reluctant to recognize the fundamental principle that stability of an international monetary system requires rates of exchange broadly corresponding to the internal purchasing-power of the different currencies. And, as we have seen in the last paragraph, the neglect of this principle had left some elements of dis-equilibrium in the new international system of money. Still worse, the fundamental conditions for the safe working of the gold standard and for stability in the value of gold itself had been disregarded in the endeavours to bring about a formal restoration of the gold standard. In consequence, the new system suffered from the outset from an instability which was to prove fatal.

A necessary pre-requisite for the stability of any

international system of money is that reasonable freedom be given to the international movement of goods, services, and capital. This had been said many times, and indeed many times acknowledged. But nations were slow in relieving the world's trade from the extraordinary obstacles that had been placed in the way of free economic intercourse. The World Economic Conference which assembled in Geneva in 1927, and whose chief aim was expected to be the restoration of more normal conditions to production and trade, was at once confronted with French proposals calculated to allow room for stronger protectionism. Only after a hard fight against these tendencies was it possible to unite the Conference on recommendations in favour of a general return to freer trade. These recommendations had a remarkably good reception from different governments, but they were never acted upon. Actual development of trade policy took the opposite direction, and thus the conditions of international trade became farther and farther removed from those required for a safe functioning of the international gold-standard system. With regard to the freedom of capital movements, the Geneva Conference was entirely negative. As a member of the Conference I made every effort to get a resolution in favour of such freedom accepted, and I followed the matter up through all the sub-committees and committees that form part of such a great conference. At every stage, however, I met with obstinate resistance from the French Delegation, and finally the recommendation was dropped. I then went to M. Loucheur and asked him the true reason for this stubborn opposition. He was reluctant to answer, but eventually I was given to understand that the French Delegation was forbidden by M. Poincaré to accept such a resolution. This illustrates how political influences could dominate the Geneva Conference in spite of its being officially constituted as a conference of independent experts who were only to give their own opinions. But the story also demonstrates how little the economic pre-requisites of monetary stability were understood even so late as in 1927.

The stability of the new gold-standard system was also threatened by disturbing monetary factors affecting the very foundations of the system. The most apparent and immediately destructive of these factors was the very one-sided distribution of the world's gold reserves, which exposed a growing number of countries to an acute shortness of gold. This maldistribution of gold was a consequence partly of the prevailing protectionism, but more directly of the huge payments on account of reparations and War debts which, in spite of all warnings from sensible economists, continued to be enforced by politicians in power.

So long as French people were willing, owing to the instability of the French franc, to maintain increasing balances abroad, and so long as Americans were willing to extend huge loans to the outside world, equilibrium in international payments could be maintained without too great difficulties. But this equilibrium was unstable and would be broken the moment that the conditions indicated ceased to be fulfilled.

In the background there was always the deficiency of the world's gold production. In fact, as we have seen (§ 2), the annual production only amounted to something like two-thirds of the normal requirements. This deficiency could temporarily be made good by withdrawal of gold coins from circulation and by other gold-economizing devices. But as the price-level in terms of gold was about 150 per cent. of the pre-War price-level there was always the danger that the supply of gold would prove insufficient to support this price-level and that the shortage of gold would enforce a prolonged process of deflation, with the effect of depressing the world's production and trade, ruining debtors, and making the burden of public debts intolerable.

Opinions were divided as to how to meet this difficulty. Some people, especially in America, regarded the prevailing price-level as in itself too high and were inclined to look upon the pre-War level as representing a 'natural' state of things to which the world would have to revert. Radical deflation was spoken of as a purging process that the world had to go through in order to regain economic health. This way was even proclaimed to be the only moral one, and all opposition was stamped as irresponsible folly or as dishonest support of a vicious speculation. However, most of the business world, as well as the majority of economists, continued to believe in the possibility, by means of a suitable restriction of the demand for gold, of maintaining the existing price-level on the basis of the available stocks of gold.

Thus the actual development, after the Genoa Conference, had brought the gold problem in its entirety more and more into the foreground, and it began to be widely felt that a thorough examination of this problem and its connexions with the great practical question of the stability of the new gold-standard system was one of urgent necessity. The Financial Committee of the League of Nations took up the matter in a report of May 1928, in which it said:

'The attention of the Financial Committee has been called to the recommendation of the Economic Consultative Committee of May 19th last, with reference to the detrimental effect upon industry, agriculture and the conditions of employment of undue fluctuations in the purchasing power of gold. The Financial Committee recognizes the great importance and interest of this subject. The financial resolutions of the Conference of Genoa were referred in 1922 to the Financial Committee by the Council, which invited the Committee to consider the methods best suited to foster monetary stability. These resolutions dealt not only with problems arising from currency fluctuations in relation to gold, but also with undue fluctuations in the purchasing power of gold itself. They contemplated, as a first stage, the stabilization of currencies in relation to gold.

'Very great progress has been made in this direction in the last few years, some countries stabilizing by independent efforts, others with the aid of international co-operation, whether through the League or not; and this first stage may now be regarded as nearing its conclusion. This gives special interest to the problems connected with undue fluctuations in the purchasing power of gold, and makes the moment opportune for a study of it. The Committee would be glad therefore, if the Council so desires, to consider to what extent and in what way the League, whose efforts have necessarily been concentrated hitherto on a contribution to the first stage of the world's post-war monetary problem, could now most usefully assist in the study and solution of the problem in this second stage.'

It may be doubted whether the long delay in taking up the question of fluctuations in the purchasing-power of gold was really necessary. Both in Brussels and Genoa this question had been contemplated in its natural and immediate connexion with the restoration of the gold standard, and it was certainly expected that the matter would be treated in the same way when it was handed over to the League of Nations. The unwarranted postponement of action in this matter had the most detrimental effects in allowing the internal instability of the new gold-standard system to develop uncontrolled until the moment when a collapse was unavoidable. The truth is that the politicians in power had so concentrated their attention upon the question of how to enforce reparations from Germany that they had no interest left for an investigation of the dangers threatening the stability of the world's monetary system; indeed, they disliked and systematically prevented any official discussion that could throw a shadow of doubt upon the wisdom of the reparations policy. Even when at last, after another year's delay, the 'Gold Delegation' was created, strong forces endeavoured to restrict its terms of reference as far as possible. In fact, the Delegation was appointed to 'examine into and report upon the causes of fluctuations in the purchasing-power of gold and their effect upon the economic life of the nations'. No reference was made here to the means for preventing such fluctuations or for mitigating their pernicious effects.

The Gold Delegation held its first meeting in August 1929 and delivered its final report in June 1932. In the meantime the very catastrophe which its work should have contributed to avert had come upon the world. The new international gold standard broke down, and in its final report the Delegation was, in the official language of the Financial Committee, 'forced to take into consideration the wider problems to which these circumstances had given rise'. This new aspect of the task belongs to the following chapter.

III

THE DISRUPTION OF THE NEW SYSTEM

§ 10. *Renewed Deflation and its Consequences*

THE building up of the new international gold-standard system had hardly been accomplished when a process of destruction began that led to its final collapse. The world-wide deflation that had been threatening for several years and against which so many grave warnings had been issued began to manifest itself in 1928.

As we have seen, France returned to the gold standard in June 1928. For this purpose the country had already accumulated gold for a couple of years and now continued these accumulations on a large scale. In the United States the boom conditions in 1928 increased the domestic demand for capital to such an extent that the country's earlier capacity for capital export was threatened. At the same time countries who had borrowed freely from America began to exhaust their capacity for borrowing, being unable any longer to offer reliable security. In consequence, the American export of capital began to run dry and the huge surplus in the American balance of payments had to be paid in gold.

The following are the figures of the gold reserves

of the United States and France for the years 1925–31 (in million dollars):[1]

	United States	*France*
1925 December	3,985	711
1926 "	4,083	711
1927 "	3,977	954
1928 "	3,746	1,254
1929 "	3,900	1,633
1930 "	4,225	2,100
1931 August	4,632	2,296

Thus in this period America had increased her gold reserves by 647 million dollars and France hers by 1,585 million dollars. Together these two countries had taken not less than 2,232 million dollars, a sum roughly corresponding to the world's total gold production in the period. In the same period some other countries, particularly Holland, Belgium, and Switzerland, considerably increased their gold reserves, with the consequence of an actual fall in the total gold reserve of the rest of the world.

This gold shortage exercised an awkward pressure on the price-levels of the different countries. According to the classical theory of the gold standard this tendency would have been counterbalanced by a rise of the price-level in the gold-receiving countries, and gradually an adjustment would have taken place without any great changes in the average world prices. But France and the United States did not use their newly

[1] *Federal Reserve Bulletin*, May 1932.

acquired gold for a corresponding credit expansion which could have brought about the desirable rise in prices. On the contrary, the price-levels were forced down even in these countries. The annual average of the American price-index (Professor Fisher) in 1925 stood at the figure 159 and in 1928 at 149. In August 1931 the index had been brought down to 105. In France the annual average reached its maximum in 1926 with the figure 703. After that time the price-level was gradually lowered and in August 1931 reached the figure 446. In other countries there had been a similar fall in prices.

Naturally, the agricultural and raw material producing countries, which as a rule were also debtor countries, were most immediately and most severely struck by this process of deflation. When prices fell these countries had to produce more and sell more in order to be able to meet their obligations. Thus markets were spoiled, producers were ruined, and the countries in question had to abandon the gold standard. The Argentine and Uruguay suspended gold payments in December 1929; Canada introduced monetary restrictions at about the same time, and in 1930 the exchanges of Brazil, Chile, Venezuela, Paraguay, Peru, Australia, and New Zealand fell below par.

Officially this destructive process is usually recorded in such a way as to give the impression that an over-production of primary commodities forced down their prices with the ultimate consequence of a general collapse of prices. But since industrial over-production is at the same time quoted as a cause of the break-down, it is difficult to accept this explanation. True, certain maladjustments between different classes of prices arose, but these discrepancies could no doubt have been ironed out by the ordinary self-regulating forces of economic life. When the *general* price-level was affected in the appalling manner described, this was essentially a *monetary* phenomenon the explanation of which can only be found in factors of a monetary nature.

The process of deflation that had been initiated by the gold accumulations of some few countries could never end so long as these countries believed that their safety required a continued accumulation of gold coupled with a continued deflation of their currencies. In the long run, however, no country can stand such a process of deflation, which is bound to ruin debtors and producers and to increase the burden of public obligations to a point at which it becomes intolerable for the tax-payers.

The American crisis that began with the collapse of the New York Stock Exchange in the autumn of 1929, and which was followed by the most violent and widespread depression in the world's economic history, can only be understood when viewed as a result of this destructive process of deflation. Numberless efforts have been made to find other explanations, evading the essential monetary nature of the catastrophe. Such explanations are very little in touch with reality, being mostly dependent upon untenable theories of over-production.[1] After the crisis the directors of the Federal Reserve System gradually relaxed their restrictive policy; but they did so only reluctantly and too slowly and never made it clear that they intended to stop the process of deflation. Still less did the system accept any responsibility in this respect.[2] Under such circumstances the general fear of a further fall in prices could not be removed and conditions both in the United States and in the world at large merely continued to deteriorate.

In 1931 the process of destruction had gone so far as to produce a tornado over the European Continent, threatening the economy of a number of countries with complete collapse. As usual on such occasions, demands for liquidity increased beyond all limits. London as the world's monetary centre was naturally exposed to tremendous pressure. The technical position of the London money-market was weak because

[1] Compare: *The Crisis in the World's Monetary System* (hereafter referred to as *Crisis*), p. 55, &c.; *Quantitative Thinking*, p. 58, &c., and *Skand. Quarterly*, October 1932.

[2] As to the nature of such responsibility see *Crisis*, p. 44, &c.

it had borrowed on short term and made long-term investments. The Bank of England and the Government tried to save the situation by means of large foreign credits. These were, however, rapidly exhausted and on Saturday, 19 September, the Bank of England applied to the Government for release from their legal obligation to sell gold under the Gold Standard Act of 1925.

Viscount Snowden in his *Autobiography* describes the events in the following way:

'The Prime Minister and I spent that week-end in London in consultation with the Bank of England and other financial bodies. We came to the conclusion that we must at once ask Parliament to suspend the gold convertibility of the currency. The amount of foreign assets held in London largely exceeded the amount of the bankers' gold. If the Bank of England in these circumstances remained under a legal obligation to pay out gold on demand the security of the currency might have disappeared.

'The next day (Monday, the 21st September), amid great excitement, I introduced into the House of Commons a Bill to suspend the Gold Standard. We were well aware that the initial effect on the exchange value of sterling might be serious, but we believed that this effect would be temporary, and that those who had confidence in sterling would not find that confidence misplaced.'

This description is very instructive. Firstly, it shows that in this case, as in so many others, the interest in maintaining gold reserves was given preference over the redeemability that these reserves were to guarantee. This experience should once and for all put an end to the old orthodox belief in gold reserves as a guarantee of redeemability. It is usually pretended that gold reserves are required for meeting emergency demands. But to this very day the world has never seen a serious emergency arise in a gold-standard country without efforts being concentrated on the protection of the gold reserves, even at the cost of sacrificing redeemability.

Secondly, Viscount Snowden's short narrative proves what little insight the authorities had at that time into the deep-seated nature of the crisis. The 'effect on the exchange value of sterling' would certainly not be 'temporary'. The international quotation of the pound had to adjust itself to the internal purchasing-power of the currency and, as gold continued to rise in value in terms of commodities, this adjustment would mean a very considerable and persistent reduction in the gold value of the pound.

When England was driven off the gold standard, smaller countries intimately connected with England by commercial relations necessarily encountered great difficulties in maintaining their currencies on a gold basis. A week after England Sweden had to leave the gold standard. The motives for exempting the Riksbank from its obligation to redeem its notes in gold were similar to those that were advanced in England: the demands for gold were so heavy that the gold reserve of the Riksbank threatened to fall below the legal minimum. Thus even in this case the maintenance of the gold reserve was considered more important than the redeemability of the currency. In Sweden, too, the suspension of gold payments was officially represented as a temporary measure of emergency, and the authorities hardly realized how much the gold value of the Swedish currency would have to sink before it was brought down to a level with the currency's internal purchasing-power.

When Sweden left the gold standard it was important that some other standard should be set up for the regulation of the Swedish currency. On being asked for my counsel I insisted upon a definite declaration to the effect that the maintenance of the internal purchasing-power of the Swedish krone as against commodities was the aim of Sweden's monetary policy. The natural fear that the abandonment of the gold standard would mean leaving the currency to the mercies of uncontrolled inflation could only be met by a declaration fixing a new standard for the regulation of the currency by the central bank. The decisions arrived at were in accordance with this view. In order to demonstrate its absolute resolve not to allow any inflation to take place the Riksbank immediately raised its rate of discount to 8 per cent. and only gradually lowered it to a more normal level. This severity evoked much criticism; at all events it had its psychological effect, and the Swedish people were soon convinced that the krone was a quite reliable currency.

The parallel events in England are well known and generally understood. The British people soon came round to the view that the pound was in safe hands and could be relied upon as a stable currency. Yet the old gold mentality remained and was constantly strengthened by the financial papers' quotations of the value of sterling in terms of 'gold shillings'. It took a long time to root out the idea that sterling was fluctuating in terms of an absolute value represented by gold, and to educate people to be content with the stability of sterling in terms of commodities.

Wherever the gold standard had to be abandoned, technical explanations, such as the financial pressure of the moment, or an unfavourable development of the balance of trade, &c., were brought into the foreground. It took some time before people began to realize that the break-down of the gold standard was the inevitable result of a fundamental disequilibrium in the world's monetary system. The increasing scarcity of the gold that was actually available for trade purposes could be met for some time by a process of deflation, bringing down the general price-level and thus raising the purchasing-power of the several currencies so as to balance the rising value of gold. But this process was extremely pernicious and must in the long run become intolerable, particularly for countries with huge public debts or with heavy commitments abroad. In addition, the tendency of strong trade unionism to defend the existing level of nominal wages made the costs of production in many countries so inflexible that further deflation appeared impossible on account of social and political considerations.

In consequence of these difficulties the international gold-standard system broke down and the very serious endeavours and sacrifices that had been made in order to reconstruct such a system were completely frustrated. What was left of the system was a torso. The small group of countries remaining 'true to gold' could not claim to represent an international gold standard: they could maintain their gold parities only by quite artificial means; and they were doomed to walk a painful road—whether long or short—towards final monetary collapse.

The lesson of all this is that the international gold-standard system is a very dangerous mechanism. The apprehensions to which France's monetary behaviour after her return to gold gave rise (§ 8) have been only too grimly confirmed. A one-sided accumulation of gold on a large scale may at any time force members of a gold-standard system to a deflation, seriously jeopardizing their whole economic life. It is possible that the whole monetary system may thereby be brought into such disequilibrium that it will simply break down and leave the world in a situation of complete monetary disorder. There must be some fault in the very method of choosing as a basis for the world's monetary system a commodity the value of which is liable to extreme and incalculable variations because it can be accumulated in unlimited quantities by those who, in a particular situation, may have the power and the desire to do so.

§ 11. *The Nature of the Crisis*

Very different views have been advanced as to the nature of the world crisis which culminated in the collapse of the international gold-standard system. The Socialists, of course, were eager to represent the crisis as the final break-down of the capitalistic system. In the appalling economic disorder that ensued a large amount of State Leadership and Control seemed to be indispensable, and the occasion was thought favourable for an agitation aiming at replacing the old social order of individual freedom by some form of authoritative 'Planning'. No matter whether a democratic or dictatorial form was deemed desirable for this régime, Socialists of all shades were united in their condemnation of the capitalistic system that had brought such disaster upon the world.

On closer analysis this must be found to be a singularly unfair verdict. In all essential points the responsibility for the collapse of the social economy lay entirely on governments, parliaments, and central banks. The entire War and the Peace Treaty, involving as it did calamitous demands for reparations and the disintegration of the international trading community, were the work of States; while some leading States and central banks were jointly responsible for the last and fatal process of deflation. Again, in the subsequent development of a super-protectionism, with the consequence of a progressive destruction of international economic relations, the active forces were governments and parliaments, sometimes with the widest support of democracy.

As to 'capitalism', the wonderful thing is that it could survive all these calamities in spite of the tremendous burdens of taxation that it had to carry; and the fact that the world economy still functions is nothing less than a triumph for the energy and the capacity for adaptation of Individual Enterprise. Before States enter further upon the path of economic regulation and guardianship they should pay more attention to the functions which they of necessity have to fulfil in economic life, and, first of all, concentrate their efforts upon creating a reliable system of money. The indispensable State activities must obviously be maintained in a fairly satisfactory manner if the so-called capitalistic system is to be able to work with full efficiency and show what it is capable of performing. Only then is a fair judgement of the value of this economic system possible.

Now, apart from the socialistic interpretation of the world crisis, there are two sharply divergent opinions as to the nature of the crisis. One school emphasizes the *monetary* nature of the destruction which has befallen the world's economy. The shortcomings of the monetary organization and administration are looked upon as the basic elements in this process. No doubt faults in the monetary system can in many cases be traced back to mistakes of a non-monetary nature, such as reparation claims and extreme protectionism, but it is thought that such influences must be analysed in their connexion with the monetary development.

The opposite school does its best to prevent this monetary character of the crisis from being brought out into the full light of day. To this end great emphasis is laid upon the *economic* nature of the crisis, and all sorts of 'maladjustments' in the world's economic life are sought for and presented as causes of the crisis. Usually, no sufficient analysis is made of the causal connexion between the different factors believed to have co-operated in producing the final catastrophe. A great many of the most heterogeneous elements are simply enumerated without any effort to co-ordinate them into a systematic explanation of what has actually happened. The effect is that the public finds itself completely bewildered and is left to draw the conclusion that the crisis is such an extremely complicated problem that no clear explanation can ever be given of it, nor even the main outlines of such an explanation. Endeavours have actually been made to represent the present crisis merely as a phase of the regular business cycle of pre-War times. This view involves the belief in the necessity for the crisis as a continuation of a movement of mathematical regularity. Such reasoning must be emphatically rejected, not only as theoretically ill-founded, but also as morally unsound, in so far as it tends to let all responsibility for what has happened vanish.

When the Gold Delegation of the League of Nations found itself in the situation of having to explain the general collapse which its investigations into the fluctuations in the purchasing-power of gold should have helped to prevent, the ideas of the members were found to be divided very much along the lines here indicated. A member of the Gold Delegation of outstanding capacity was, from the very beginning, Sir Henry Strakosch, and he performed singularly good service in producing a clear and well-documented analysis of the essentially monetary nature of the crisis. He was supported by a few other members, including myself, but the majority of the Delegation proved to be strangely incapable of appreciating any such analysis, and all hopes for a unanimous report had to be abandoned.

In January 1932 the minority met to prepare a report of their own. As to the causes of the crisis, this report comes to the conclusion which is summarized in the following words:

'The breakdown of the gold standard must therefore be regarded as the combined result of the obligation to pay reparations and war debts on the one side, and the unwillingness of the receiving countries to receive payment in the form of goods and services on the other.

'It remains to be explained why this huge accumulation of gold did not produce an increase in the supply of means of payment and therefore a rise in internal prices in the receiving countries. According to the classical doctrine of the functioning of the gold standard, such a rise in prices would have been the automatic effect of the inflow of gold, and this effect would have checked the inflow and eventually caused a reversal of the movement. However, both in France and the United States, the gold was not used for any such purpose, but was simply buried in the vaults of the Central Banks. Not only was the level of prices of these countries not raised, but was actually lowered as the price level fell in the rest of the world.

'It is a widespread belief that the present crisis is merely a phase of a cyclic movement of business activity—a crisis, therefore, which has to be regarded as the inevitable result of the forces of instability assumed to be inherent in the present organisation of the world's economy. This belief stands in the way of a true analysis of the development that has led to the catastrophe in which the world is now involved. It prevents those who hold it from appreciating the real causes of these disastrous developments. We think it is of the highest importance to discard such vague conceptions and thus to clear the ground for an objective investigation of the present situation in the light of distinct and clearly traceable facts.'

This statement does not seem to leave much to be desired in condensed lucidity or logical conclusiveness.

The 'Note of Dissent', which was signed by M. Albert Jansen, Sir Reginald Mant, and Sir Henry Strakosch and published together with the final report of the Gold Delegation,[1] begins with the following criticism of the views of the majority:

'In the first place, we must dissociate ourselves entirely from Section IV of the report, headed "The Breakdown of the International Money System", in which an analysis is given of the causes which led to the recent abandonment of the gold standard by so many countries. This analysis suggests that the crisis was the direct result of various economic maladjustments arising from the war and from war and post-war inflation. In support of this view our colleagues refer to profound changes in the structure and localisation of industry, to its elaborate and rigid organisation, to cartelisation,

[1] Geneva, June 1932.

attempts at price control, pools, valorisation schemes and the like, and to tariffs, prohibitions, and bounties. It is claimed that these conditions caused maladjustments in economic factors and processes and that there resulted a general instability which the international gold standard was not able to withstand. Hence its breakdown.

'No concrete evidence of any kind—statistical or otherwise—is adduced in support of this analysis; in particular, no evidence is adduced to show that these factors were of so exceptionally intense a character as not to be amenable to the self-righting forces of economic life and particularly to the potent forces of adjustment which the operation of the gold standard of necessity imposes upon the countries adhering to it. Nor does the report attempt to describe the process by which these disequilibria brought about the violent rise in the value of gold in recent times.'

This gives a good picture of the sort of mental resistance that must be overcome before any profitable examination of the crisis can begin. The first condition for any productive work in this field is that the break-down of the world's monetary system shall be recognized as a *monetary* phenomenon that requires a *monetary* explanation.

§ 12. *Remedies Proposed*

Amidst a great revolution in the world's monetary system we are forced earnestly to ask ourselves: What should be the objective of monetary policy? What can we rightly demand from a sound system of money? These questions need answers on broad practical lines. We are faced with an urgent necessity for monetary reconstruction, and our task is to draw up proposals that will work, and work better than the system that has collapsed.

In such a situation we can always expect an army of critics to march up, eager to find faults with any positive solution on the ground that it does not represent the theoretical ideal. The ideals put forth by such critics are usually rather arbitrary, and often contradict one another. The result is that the whole discussion is lost in endless controversies about trifles and theoretical refinements and that the public is left in a deplorable confusion of thought and without any guidance in regard to practical action.

In the Gold Delegation we saw a good deal of such 'contributions' to our work and the majority report shows many traces of their influence. In contrast, it makes a refreshing impression when the 'Note of Dissent', signed by the minority, states in plain terms that '*the prime objective of monetary policy should be stability in the general level of wholesale commodity prices*'.[1]

There are always numberless objections raised to such a simple and definite programme. It is pointed out that the usual indexes of the level of wholesale commodity prices by no means furnish an exact

[1] *Report of the Gold Delegation*, Geneva, 1932, p. 67.

measure of the fluctuations of that level, and that index numbers must be constructed on a much broader basis and calculated with more refined methods if they are to serve as a standard of monetary stability. In this connexion exaggerated and theoretically unsound claims have been brought forward. On the other hand, opinions differ even as to the desirability of maintaining the general level of wholesale prices constant. Some authors propose that this level should be lowered in the same proportion as technical progress reduces 'costs of production'.[1] There are also advocates of the opposite view that the general price-level ought regularly to rise in order to give constant encouragement to production. Some authors even oppose the very idea of stability on the ground that fluctuations of the price-level have a particularly stimulating effect on enterprise and economic leadership! Others go so far as to assert that any policy aiming at stability of the general price-level is a dangerous experiment. In a world in which everything else is mobile, they tell us, the inevitable result of such one-sided stabilization will be an explosion! How these critics can recommend the gold standard, which fixes the price of gold in a constantly fluctuating economic system, remains to be explained. To all these very clever and very contradictory arguments is added the view that the development of the general

[1] The fallacy of this reasoning is demonstrated in *Crisis*, p. 49.

price-level ought to be controlled in such a way as to do the highest possible 'justice' to all the divergent interests concerned. Of course, the interpretation of the concept 'justice' gives rise to new controversies, which will doubtless one day fill libraries.

A discussion on such lines can go on *ad infinitum* without leading to any result. It falls entirely outside the scope of the practical task that has to be accomplished. Having realized that gold is a very unsatisfactory standard of value we have to find an essentially broader basis for monetary stability. Then, instead of fixing the price of one single commodity, as we do in the gold-standard system, we turn to an approximate fixing of the aggregate price of a great number of important commodities, or, what amounts to the same thing, we choose an index for the general level of commodity prices and decide to regard the invariability of this index as our standard of monetary stability. Of course, such a solution involves a certain amount of arbitrariness, but it marks an immense practical step forward: a monetary system based upon such a standard would possess much greater stability than the gold-standard system. For the world's economic life this new stability would be a blessing beyond all compare. For the present we must be content with that and leave it to doctors' dissertations in a coming century to find out the shortcomings of our system. It is, I repeat, our task to find a standard of stability that will serve its practical purpose and—what is very important—at the same time one that is simple enough to be understood by everybody and to have some reasonable prospect of being accepted internationally.

The choice of a new standard does not necessarily involve a complete dethronement of gold. To many people a formal maintenance of the gold standard seems desirable. This must entail that the value of gold itself be systematically regulated so as to remain constant according to the accepted standard of stability. Indeed, this is the real content of all the programmes that are now in the forefront of international discussion for a 'modernized gold standard' and which aim at preventing fluctuations in the value of gold by means of a gold-economizing policy and other similar devices. But at the moment such programmes are accepted, gold ceases to be the ultimate standard of value. It may remain an auxiliary standard, but only as long as the policy of stabilizing the value of gold in terms of the new commodity standard succeeds. In the following pages we shall see how completely the old concept of the gold standard has been revolutionized under the influence which these ideas have won in the last few years. We shall also see how the desirability of using gold as such an auxiliary standard has been impaired by recent experiences.

The minority of the Gold Delegation in their 'Note of Dissent' still entertain the hope that it will be possible to reconstruct an international gold-standard system. But they are very outspoken as to the conditions that must be fulfilled in order to achieve this purpose. They say:

> 'If the gold standard is once more to be restored as an international standard, the real difficulties of such a task must be clearly faced.
>
> 'The first requisite for the restoration of the gold standard must obviously be the removal of the forces which have caused it to break down.'

They proceed to formulate four essential conditions which must be fulfilled, and they then conclude:

> 'Unless these conditions are fulfilled, a general return to the gold standard is not possible, and, even if it were temporarily possible, it would be undesirable and dangerous. There would be a risk of further deflation and of a consequent aggravation of the present economic depression. It is pretty certain that countries which had returned to the gold standard without the necessary safeguards for its stability would soon be driven off it again. Thus the international gold standard would not offer that security for international trade, the establishment of which is the very purpose of that standard.'

The majority of the Gold Delegation were satisfied with stating in general terms that 'at the present stage of world economic development the gold standard remains the best available monetary mechanism'. This recommendation has often been quoted when later international conferences and bodies have wished to make their confession of faith in the gold standard. Such confessions are indeed of very little value so long as the chief conditions for a return to the gold standard and for its stability are neglected and so long as no understanding is reached on the vital question of the ultimate standard by which the stability of the gold standard should be judged. The warning of the minority of the Gold Delegation against the dangers of a premature return to the gold standard without the necessary safeguards has proved to be very much to the point. This has best been seen when on later occasions lighthearted recommendations for a return to gold have been accepted in the hope that unanimity could most easily be secured if all cumbersome conditions were left out and the programme were reduced to a mere wishy-washy statement.

For my own part I was perhaps a shade more sceptical as to the prospect of a return to the gold standard than even those of my colleagues on the Gold Delegation who signed the minority 'Note of Dissent'. I was unable to attend the last meeting of the Gold Delegation as I had accepted an invitation from Oxford to act as Rhodes Memorial Lecturer during the Trinity Term of 1932. For this reason, and also because the final report of the Gold Delegation had mixed up right and wrong 'in such a bewildering way that it is extremely difficult to state all the reservations to which an endorsement of the report would be subject', I found myself unable to sign that report and had to give my views in a very condensed 'Memorandum of Dissent'[1]). In order to show how I viewed the problem at that time I should like to reprint here the latter part of this memorandum:

'Turning our attention to this problem of the future, we have first to observe that the value of gold has become exposed to so many incalculable influences that it is impossible now in any true sense to speak of gold as a fixed standard of value. The destruction of the old gold-standard system has, in fact, gone much further than a temporary abandonment of the gold standard by some few countries would denote. We are faced actually with the complete destruction of the essential quality that made gold an acceptable standard of value for an international system of money. It is necessary to keep this fact in mind, if we want to form a clear judgement on the possibility of a restoration of an international gold-standard system. Such a restoration would, at any rate, require the fulfilment of a number of essential conditions among which the following should be mentioned here: a great reduction in the value of gold, a radical redistribution of the world's gold reserves, the resumption of a systematic gold economising policy, cancellation of all claims on repara-

[1] *Report of the Gold Delegation*, p. 74.

tion and war-debt payments, definite guarantees against the repetition of such extraordinary demands for gold as have occurred during the last few years and, finally, restoration of a reasonable freedom of international trade and of international capital movements.

'Whatever the prospects of such reforms may be, it seems quite clear, at the very best, several years must elapse before a restoration of an international gold-standard system can be seriously contemplated. Any premature attempt to use an occasional opportunity for a formal restoration of the gold standard, without the necessary safeguards for its stability, would be extremely dangerous and must be expected to lead to new disasters. If we want to construct a new gold-standard system, we must take care that the foundations are laid with sufficient solidity.

'In the meantime, we have to make the best of our existing currencies. The countries off the gold standard have to secure the greatest possible stability for the internal purchasing power of their paper currencies. Before doing this, however, they must first raise their price level at least some halfway up to the price level of 1929. Thereafter, the stabilization should be carried out. In order to secure the greatest possible stability to the exchanges between the paper currencies, it seems necessary that Great Britain should take the lead with the aim of creating a 'Sterling Group'. The different currencies of this group should be regulated so as to remain in a certain parity with sterling. Within such a 'Sterling Group', it would be possible to develop a sound international trade of some stability.

'For the countries remaining on the gold standard the most

urgent aim is to force down the value of gold. They could do this themselves by reducing their monetary demands for gold, and the paper-standard countries could contribute to that end by selling gold which they have no longer any reason to keep.

'It is an open question whether it will be possible in the future to restore the gold standard as an international monetary system. It is quite possible that the difficulties will prove insuperable, and that the paper-standard system will attain such a stability as to become generally acceptable. Even if we believe in the restoration of the gold standard, and are prepared to make the most serious efforts and sacrifices to this end, the creation of a group of paper standards of the highest possible stability is a preliminary stage which cannot be omitted. For the moment, the paper countries must concentrate their attention entirely upon this aim. Their agreement on such a policy would at once open possibilities for a new development of trade and production and should therefore be the most immediate concern of the economic policy of these countries.

'From this analysis, it is clear that the problem of monetary reconstruction has now taken an aspect which places it far beyond the domain of the questions which the Gold Delegation was called upon to examine. The world's monetary problem will henceforth have to be discussed on far broader lines.'

§ 13. *Sterling off Gold*

When in September 1931 Great Britain abandoned the gold standard, and when therefore the pound ceased to be the equivalent of a gold sovereign, it was natural that people should ask: What is a pound? If no exact definition could be given, people would at least inquire: What are the general principles according to which the value of the pound is going to be regulated for the future? What is the policy of the British monetary authorities, and what responsibility are they prepared to assume for its effectual realization? Such questions would be asked not only in Great Britain but in every part of the British Empire, and, in addition, in every country in the world that had abandoned the gold standard and wanted to link its currency to the pound sterling.

The British authorities have been rather reluctant to give any definite answer to these questions. In the House of Commons, however, after the first feelings of consternation had been overcome, an increasing interest in the matter manifested itself, and in the summer session of 1932 several important debates on the monetary policy of the country took place. In May 1932 I was invited by the Conservative Party Finance Committee of the House to deliver an address[1] on the monetary situation, and I used the opportunity for defining what I considered ought to be the objective of British monetary policy. I said: 'In the long run this objective can naturally consist only in a certain stability of the internal purchasing-power

[1] Printed by the *Kentish Times*, Sidcup, Kent, under the title: 'The Destruction of the World's Monetary System'.

of the pound as against commodities: that is to say, the aim must be sought in establishing a certain stability of the general level of wholesale commodity prices.'

First, however,

'*it is necessary to raise the price level.* The present bottom-level is certainly not suitable as a basis for the new monetary system. We must reach a price level more nearly adapted to fixed charges and relatively fixed wages. That is to say: a raising of the present price level to at least half-way towards the price level of 1929 has to be made the first point in the monetary programme. This task may be accomplished within a comparatively short time, and thereafter the programme must be to keep the price level constant.

'On the basis of such a programme it would doubtless be very easy to come to an agreement with other paper standard countries and secure their co-operation for monetary stability. Thus *A Sterling Group* could be formed where each participating country had its own currency but where all the other currencies were so regulated as to keep sterling exchange stable.'

With regard to the Imperial Conference that was to take place in Ottawa in the following summer I suggested that it is

'*quite impossible for Great Britain to go to Ottawa not being prepared to tell the other participants in the Conference what the pound sterling is going to represent in the future, or what are the fundamental principles underlying Great Britain's actual monetary policy.* An expert discussion of these important questions and of the possibilities of forming a Sterling Group must be regarded as an essential part of the preparations for the Imperial Conference.

'England should never forget how great the interests are which are bound up with the solution of her own monetary problem. The formation of a Sterling Group of paper currencies, rationally regulated, for safeguarding stability would secure for Great Britain an independence of arbitrary and haphazard influences and of endeavours to exploit monetary resources for political ends, and would thus finally break the *intolerable power* that has been built on huge accumulations of gold reserves.

'As a leader of the Sterling Group, Great Britain would again acquire the authority and lead to which she is so justly entitled in international affairs.'

In an address which I delivered to the Royal Institute of International Affairs on 16 June[1] I further developed these ideas in the following words:

'Going off the gold standard is obviously a negative measure. It must be completed by a more positive move—namely, the choosing of another standard for the pound sterling. Obviously you cannot be without any standard. It is impossible to say that you reckon in sterling, if you do not know what sterling is, if you do not know what sterling is going to be, if you have no idea of the factors influencing the value of sterling.' . . .

'Therefore the first positive step which you have to take is to make a definition of the sterling standard. The authorities

[1] *International Affairs*, London, Sept. 1932, vol. xi, no. 5.

of this country should tell the people and the rest of the world what this pound sterling standard is going to be for the future. Again I say that perhaps we cannot ask them to give exact figures with decimals, but we can ask them for general principles as to how they want to regulate the value of sterling. I think there is no other answer to that question than that the pound sterling must for the future have a definite purchasing power in terms of commodities within the country.'

With regard to a forthcoming international monetary conference and the necessity for Great Britain to take the lead I had some words to say which, in the light of what actually happened later, it may be of some interest to read again:

'There has been some talk in the last few days about coming to an agreement with the United States. That would in itself be excellent. But when it is suggested that there should be for this purpose an international conference on the reconstruction of the world's monetary system, I want to say that the preliminary condition that must be fulfilled for such an undertaking is an understanding between this country and the United States, and that does not require a formal conference at all. If you can get some American experts over here to talk with your experts, and if you can unite on a definite policy for raising the price level in both countries that would give you immense authority.' . . .

'You have never in history had a better opportunity for leadership than you have now. You can build up a sterling group, you can get sound co-operation from the United

States. They are already prepared for such a raising of prices, if they could only find a reasonable programme and have a definite guarantee against its misuse. That is the way in which I think we can solve the problem. We cannot attain anything by calling international conferences without preparing for them. What would a big international conference about the question of the world's monetary and economic system do? It is very probable that the question of the general restoration of the gold standard would be put in the forefront, which would be fatal.'

According to the 'Summary of Discussion' on my address Sir Basil Blackett further emphasized the need for Government leadership. He developed this point as follows:

'There seemed to be no currency policy in Great Britain. In response to pressure in the House of Commons, the Government had said that its policy was not to return to the gold standard yet, that it wished to see prices rise and did not wish to see the exchange rise, but on no occasion had any positive policy been suggested. The policy of Great Britain should be to state definitely that she wanted a stable price level in the future which would not expose the world again to the disastrous consequences of boom and slump, because the yard-stick was altering all the time.'

In the Finance Bill of 1932 the Government asked for a sum of 150 million pounds for creating an 'Exchange Equalization Account'. At first this sensational proposal was received by the country with astonishingly little hesitation and with no serious inquiry. In subsequent debates in the House of Commons, however, a more critical attitude was taken up. When the House sat in Committee on 25 May it was pointed out that a programme of stabilization necessarily presupposed a clear definition of the monetary policy of the country. If the object of the account was to check undue fluctuations in the exchange value of sterling the obvious answer was, in the words of Mr. Mabane, that fluctuations are necessarily relative. If sterling fluctuates, it must fluctuate in terms of something else. It may be intended to prevent fluctuations in terms of gold; or the object may be to prevent fluctuations in terms of commodities. 'We do not know', another member, Mr. Boothby, said, 'what is the ultimate objective of the Government, what is their real monetary policy. They have been very firm in their refusal to give the House or the Committee information as to their ultimate aims.'

The strongest opposition was raised against any contemplated or possible return to an uncontrolled gold standard. Fears were expressed lest the Equalization Account might be used for stabilizing the pound in terms of a foreign gold currency—which was tantamount to a return to the gold standard. Major Elliot, the Financial Secretary, had to assure the House on behalf of the Government 'that the Government have no intention whatever of going back to gold, at any rate while gold prices behave as they are doing now'. He added that 'there are many other subjects of great interest . . . to discuss'. The suggestion of the Financial Secretary that 'we ought to get this out of the way and pass on to more important topics' was most emphatically opposed by Mr. Churchill in words which still have the same outstanding significance as they had at that moment: 'There are no more important topics. Search the world and you will not find a topic more important than this grave, grim money problem.' After having been reminded by Sir Robert Horne that 'he must recognize, and that the Government must recognize, that there is a very strong feeling in the House on this question', Major Elliot in the name of the Government again gave the assurance, 'that they have no intention whatever, as long as gold behaves as it is doing, of returning to the Gold Standard'.

This was of course a rather meagre answer that did not define in any way the positive policy of the Government in regard to the monetary problem. In the debate in the House on 9 June a strong appeal was made to the Government to inform the House of the monetary policy it was pursuing. If a fund were created in order to stabilize the value of the pound sterling there must be some definite objectives for the administration of this fund. The Government ought to announce these objectives and make it clear that Great Britain had a distinct aim of her own in her monetary policy. The Government was repeatedly called upon in this way to give a clear lead to the world. Such a resolute action would doubtless greatly influence the development in other countries and would particularly be of help to the international conference which at that time was thought to be imminent. The Government, however, were most reluctant to commit themselves to any programme of such definiteness, and all that came out—and even that only in an indirect way—was that the Chancellor favoured a rise of the general level of commodity prices to be followed by its stabilization.

These two points were no doubt excellent as principles and would have served well as a basis for a monetary programme had the Chancellor more positively and definitely pledged himself to them and had he not made the reservation that 'I had rather stated aims than committed myself to saying that it would be possible on all occasions to achieve those aims'. This reservation was the natural outcome of a failure to recognize the essentially monetary nature of the problem of the price-level. The Chancellor further weakened his declaration when he emphasized his dependence upon the connexion between sterling prices and gold prices. Such a connexion is of course necessary if a definite gold parity is maintained. But the very advantage of leaving the gold standard should be to secure for the country independence in regulating its internal price-level in accordance with its own interests. The open acknowledgement of such freedom of action, however, must needs involve the acceptance of the corresponding responsibility, and that the authorities at the time were extremely unwilling to assume.

When the Exchange Equalization Fund was proposed, as well as on several later occasions, I expressed grave doubts as to the usefulness of such a fund. Even now, in spite of the experiment being widely regarded as a success, I still remain equally sceptical. Such a fund cannot possibly be administered without any idea of what, at any particular moment, ought to be the exchange value of the currency. Such knowledge obviously presupposes that the authorities have made up their mind at least as to the meaning of the word 'exchange': Sterling may be exchanged for quite a number of other currencies or commodities, and it is therefore imperative to state what exchange is meant before any form of exchange stabilization can be contemplated. As long as this question is left open there is always room for widely different interpretations of the meaning of stabilization and for corresponding influences on actual monetary policy. Now, I think it cannot be doubted that stabilization in terms of gold has carried great weight in the administration of the British currency, and that, in consequence, the existence of the Exchange Equalization Fund has had a certain tendency towards linking sterling to gold. In so far as this is the case, Great Britain has not gained full advantage from leaving the gold standard. Sterling has remained so bound to gold as to prevent British monetary policy from attaining, to any appreciable extent, its avowed objective of raising sterling prices.

When the Imperial Economic Conference met at Ottawa in July 1932 the monetary problem was generally felt to be of predominant importance. The leader of the Australian Delegation, Mr. Bruce, introduced his statement before the Monetary Committee with the following words: 'There is no question of greater interest to Australia at the present Conference than that of action to bring about a higher price-level and stability of exchange. Unless an increase in commodity prices can be achieved it is difficult to see how the present financial and economic system of the world can be maintained.' Sir George Schuster on behalf of India said: 'We need above everything a substantial and early rise in prices.' It was generally expected that Great Britain would take the lead in such a monetary reform. Sir George Schuster said: 'We recognize that a rise in world prices to be brought about by international co-operation is the ultimate ideal, but, short of this, we believe that a rise in sterling prices extending throughout the sterling area would not only bring us great immediate benefits, but would probably by its own stimulus and examples lead to a general movement throughout the world.' Mr. Bruce expressed doubts as to the effectivity of an international conference, but he said: 'I suggest there are other ways of achieving our objective than by such a Conference. If a definite lead were given at the present time I am certain that it would be followed by other countries. Great Britain is obviously best equipped to give that lead.' And again: 'The influence of action by Great Britain, however, cannot be exaggerated. We trust that Great Britain will make a definite declaration of her policy and give to us and to the whole world the lead which she alone can give.'

The Chancellor of the Exchequer was, however, equally reluctant to meet these expectations as he had been in his attitude towards the House of Commons. True, he expressed a desire to see wholesale sterling prices rise. He very much detracted from the importance of this declaration, however, by adding: 'The best condition for this would be a rise in gold prices, and the absence of a rise in gold prices inevitably imposes limitations on what can be done for sterling. A rise in prices cannot be effected by monetary action alone, since various other factors, which have combined to bring about the present depression, must also be modified or removed before a remedy is assured.' When Mr. Chamberlain had to account for these other factors he failed to give them their right place as elements in the necessary monetary explanation of an essentially monetary phenomenon, such as the movement of the general price-level. He quite rightly referred to reparations and War debts, to political insecurity and to economic disequilibria, but he found such an enumeration sufficient to prove that the problem of the price-level was not merely a monetary one. So long as the analysis of the causal connexions is omitted in this manner it is obviously impossible to come to a true understanding of the revolution that has taken place in the purchasing-power of money and therefore also impossible to find the true remedies for the monetary disorders. The Chancellor's reference to the limitations which his dependence on gold prices imposed upon him is easily explained by his expressing, on behalf of the United Kingdom Delegation, the 'desire to see the utmost possible stability of exchange rates both between those currencies within the Empire which are based on sterling and also between sterling and gold'.

The economic means by which the Chancellor proposed to raise the price-level are characteristic. He wanted to restrict the supply of the great primary commodities, and he suggested that it was better for this purpose to regulate production in the Empire rather than importation into Great Britain, and he meant that 'the Empire would thereby have offered to the world that lead which is so frequently called for'. Surely, if the means of rescuing the world from a depression caused by a violent process of deflation is thought to consist in a general curtailment of world production, there can be no hope of recovery. Those who have emphasized the need for monetary reconstruction take a radically different view of the matter. They think that the world's supply of money, and its monetary machinery in general, must be adapted to a growing productive capacity; and not that capacity should be cut down to suit inefficient monetary organization or narrow ideas about the aims and the efficacy of monetary policy.

The resolutions of the Ottawa Conference on monetary matters were of necessity kept down to the level of the recommendations of the British Delegation and probably far from satisfied the expectations of the other countries of the Commonwealth. Not even on the question of forming a sterling bloc was any substantial progress made. The statement that 'the Conference recognizes the value of the countries within the Commonwealth whose currencies are linked to sterling maintaining stability between their exchange rates and looks to a rise in the general level of wholesale prices as the most desirable means for facilitating this result' was certainly valuable, but it was weakened by the failure of the Conference to recognize the necessity of securing for this sterling bloc the necessary independence from gold.

The Conference deliberately limited its action by referring to 'the fact that the question is shortly to be discussed at an international conference'. The result of the Ottawa Conference with regard to the monetary problem was a postponement of all action until the International Conference at last assembled in London in June of the following year.

IV

POSTPONEMENT OF MONETARY REFORM

§ 14. *The Abandonment of Reparations*

WHEN politicians find expert economic advice inconvenient they usually take refuge in charging economists with perpetual disagreement and failure to give authoritative and reliable guidance as to practical action. However, on vital questions economists have frequently showed such unanimity in their condemnation of cherished political fallacies that the leaders of nations would have done well to let the warnings of economic science temper their trust in power. In no case has the reluctance to take advice been more conspicuous than in the question of reparations and War debts. The searching criticism to which this policy was from the outset exposed by Mr. Keynes will for ever stand as a monument to the usefulness of sound economic analysis. Most economists of any standing have since that time adopted a similar attitude, though of course they have revealed various shades of judgement. To the politicians who wanted payments this criticism was most unwelcome, and the verdict of the economists was put aside as irrelevant in a case which power ought to decide and in which economists should only have to give subordinate technical advice. For my own part, I have throughout all the different stages of the struggle over reparations and War-debt payments striven to demonstrate the impossibility of fulfilling the claims and the disastrous consequences to world economy which must follow upon any endeavours to enforce payments. The politicians' usual answer was that such criticism was evidence of an intolerable arrogance on the part of economic science. It is a gloomy consolation now that the predicted disaster has actually come over the world in the shape of a violent and prolonged economic crisis, fraught with incalculable social and political consequences.

The financial hurricane that passed over the European Continent in the early summer of 1931 revealed to every one with any economic sense that Germany could no longer continue to pay reparations. President Hoover drew the conclusion from this fact in his well-meant, but not very thoroughly considered, proposal for a one-year moratorium. In incurable blindness France blocked the plan with endless objections, and the only result was increased confusion with the obvious danger of general collapse. In this desperate situation expert advice was at last appealed to, and in August 1931 an Expert Conference was arranged in Basle, only to be followed by a new one at the same place in December. This Conference finally made it clear that the whole reparations policy would have to be abandoned. The credit for this decisive step forward in the diagnosis of the world's economic disease was due chiefly to the collaboration of two neutral experts, Mr. Collijn of Holland and Mr. Rydbeck of Sweden, with the British representative, Sir Walter Layton.

Now one would have thought that the time was ripe for action. But the politicians needed another half-year's postponement, and not until July 1932 could the Political Conference assemble in Lausanne that was to mark the end of reparations, and, ultimately, the end of other War debts.

No doubt the claimants had to make a considerable sacrifice at Lausanne, but it was more a sacrifice of ideas and illusions than of realities. In fact, the claimants themselves, by a mistaken policy carried on ever since the War in defiance of all scientific advice, had rendered payments impossible. However, when at last the decisive sacrifice was made, sensible men should have been eager to harvest the natural reward, i.e. to stop the principal economic injury that had been caused by the War-debts policy. Clearly, this was the world-wide process of deflation. However, the politicians were not yet ready to make decisions on such an important and, to them, curiously unfamiliar subject, and again they resorted to postponement. It was thought that the monetary question ought to be considered at a great international conference, and Lausanne ended with an invitation to the League of Nations to convoke a World Conference 'to decide upon the measures to solve the other economic and financial difficulties which are responsible for, and may prolong, the present world crisis'.

§ 15. *The Preparatory Commission*

In the autumn of 1932 the League of Nations constituted a 'Preparatory Commission of Experts with the task of drawing up a Draft Annotated Agenda' for the forthcoming Monetary and Economic Conference in London. This task was completed in January 1933 and a 'Draft Annotated Agenda' to serve as a sort of programme for the London Conference was transmitted to the League of Nations.

This important document was introduced by a description, in a most concentrated form, of the actual situation. Those who may be inclined to believe that such strong words as 'a coming catastrophe' and 'a break-down of the world's economy threatening our whole civilization' are to be taken as rhetorical exaggerations, merely used in my exposition to stimulate the reader's attention, ought to read this quite objective statement of facts. For the generation now growing up without personal remembrance of the misery into which the world's economy had fallen in the beginning of the thirties it will be of the highest value to have this document before them.

For these reasons I think it is worth while to reprint it here:

'Before setting forth the problems which require solution, we wish to call attention to the gravity of the situation with which the world is confronted.

'Unemployment has recently been estimated by the International Labour Office as involving at least thirty million workers. Even this huge total, which does not include the workers' families or other dependants, is probably an underestimate. The burden of suffering and demoralisation resulting from unemployment of such proportions is appalling.

'Wholesale commodity prices—expressed in gold—have declined since October 1929 by roughly a third; raw material prices on the average by 50 to 60 per cent. In the middle of December, at Winnipeg, the price of wheat fell to the lowest level recorded in any primary market for wheat during the past four centuries. Such price-declines have produced profound disturbances in the economic system. They have thrown completely out of adjustment prevailing costs of the various factors of production, have made business enterprise generally unremunerative, and have seriously disorganised practically all the world markets.

'World stocks of agricultural products and of other raw materials continue to accumulate. The index of world stocks for 1932 was double that for 1925. Huge accumulations thus overhang some of the principal markets and burden the processes of orderly price readjustment.

'Industrial production has been drastically curtailed, particularly in those trades producing capital equipment. The depths which have been reached in some instances are illustrated by the position of the United States steel industry, which, at the close of 1932, was operating at only 10 per cent. of capacity.

'The international flow of goods, hindered by currency disorders and restricted by a multiplicity of new governmental interventions, has been reduced to incredibly low levels. The total value of world trade in the third quarter of 1932 was only about one-third of that in the corresponding period of 1929. The fall during the three-year period was continuous.

'Moreover, the quantum of goods in foreign trade appears to have fallen by at least 25 per cent.; by far the largest fall on record.

'As a result of price-declines and the fall in the volume of production and trade, national incomes in many countries have fallen, it is estimated, by more than 40 per cent. The revenues of Governments, as a consequence, have suffered sharp reductions, while expenditures have shown no corresponding decline. The inevitable result has been a series of budget deficits which, in some cases, have reached unprecedented proportions.

'Only a handful of countries now retain free and uncontrolled gold-standard currency systems. Almost half the countries of the world are off the gold standard, and, in some forty countries, exchange restrictions have been imposed.

'Currency disorganisation, price-declines, curtailment of trade have thrown into sharp relief the vast and difficult problems of indebtedness with which many, if not most, countries are confronted. As matters now stand, there are countries the total value of whose export trade has fallen below the sums required for external debt service alone.

'Facts such as these indicate the extremities to which the forces of disintegration have already carried the economic and financial world. Further losses of ground cannot be contemplated without the gravest forebodings. Happily, in some quarters, there have recently been certain auguries of improvement. Thus security markets in almost every country have for several months past shown some resistance, despite discouragements. In the set-back which followed the slight revival after Lausanne, the security markets, unlike the commodity markets, did not lose all the gains that had been made. It is evident that more favourable monetary conditions, technical economic readjustments and reviving confidence are being currently interpreted by those who assume the risks of investment as affording the possibility of a genuine change for the better in the economic situation.

'Nevertheless, recovery will be halting and restricted if unaccompanied by broad measures of reconstruction. Three years of world-wide dislocation have generated a vast network of restraints upon the normal conduct of business. In the field of international trade, prohibitions, quotas, clearing agreements, exchange restrictions—to mention only some of the most widely employed forms of regulation—throttle business enterprise and individual initiative. Defensively indeed, and in many instances forced by unavoidable monetary and financial emergencies, these measures have developed into a state of virtual economic warfare. It is not only in the field of trade that this tension exists. In the difficult sphere of international monetary and currency relations and in the world capital markets, free international co-operation has given place to complex and harassing regulations designed to safeguard national interests. If a full and durable recovery is to be effected, this prevailing conflict of national economies must be resolved.

'The measures to be adopted to this end constitute the problem which the Governments must shortly face in London. In essence, the necessary programme is one of economic disarmament. In the movement towards economic reconciliation, the armistice was signed at Lausanne; the London Conference must draft the Treaty of Peace. Failure in this critical undertaking threatens a world-wide adoption of ideals of national self-sufficiency which cut unmistakably athwart the lines of economic development. Such a choice would shake the whole system of international finance to its foundations, standards of living would be lowered and the social system as we know it could hardly survive. These developments, if they occur, will be the result, not of any inevitable natural law, but of the failure of human will and intelligence to devise the necessary guarantees of political and economic international order. The responsibility of Governments is clear and inescapable.'

The 'comprehensive programme of world reconstruction' which the Commission proposed was hardly as lucid and valuable as this introduction. The Commission was a rather one-sided representation of the views on monetary stability prevailing in the few remaining gold-standard countries. The opposite school, which considered stability of currencies in terms of purchasing-power as against commodities the true foundation of the world's monetary system, was not represented at all, economic science was almost excluded; and, in particular, none of the leading British economists had been admitted.

The programme drawn up by the Commission bears the stamp of this one-sided choice of its members. The recommendations of the majority of the Gold Delegation were uncritically endorsed, and the restoration of the gold standard was taken as a self-evident part of any programme for recovery and, indeed, as a *sine qua non* of any further discussion. No doubt the Agenda contained many excellent remarks and recommendations, and, in particular, it recognized the necessity both for a rise in prices and for a subsequent stabilization of the price-level; but the whole matter was looked upon from the point of view of the gold-standard countries. *They* should pursue a policy calculated to promote a recovery of prices. Other countries were advised not to 'depreciate' unduly the external value of their currencies, as such behaviour might hamper the recovery of prices in gold countries. This is typical of the gold mentality. In France a fall of sterling in terms of francs is constantly represented as a depreciation of sterling. It never occurs to this school that the movement may equally well be described as an appreciation of gold and of gold-standard currencies in terms of sterling, and that sterling from the point of view of purchasing-power may have the better right to the distinction of being classified as a 'stable currency'. It is characteristic that the programme did not contemplate a rise of prices in paper standards. Under such circumstances it was obviously impossible for the Commission properly to expound the need for a *general* rise of prices or for a resolute policy of *reflation*, stopping further deflation and remedying the worst evils caused by the senseless deflation that had taken place since 1929. Moreover, the Commission's attitude in favour of a rise of prices lost half its value for the purpose of monetary reconstruction when the programme adhered to the confused idea criticized above that 'one method of raising prices is to limit supply'.

Everybody must have known that the views in different countries on these matters were widely divergent. The Commission, however, obviously thought it their duty to formulate a programme that could be unanimously accepted—one in which any possible controversy was bridged over by obscure and non-committal phrases. This way of treating controversial questions has been the curse of all international conferences ever since the War. Sincere international co-operation is possible only if the different standpoints are clearly stated. The very necessity for making such a statement is of immense importance, especially in the economic field, since it compels the parties to give their vague and often rather confused ideas a distinct meaning and a logical consistency. The artificial clouding of issues which aims at hiding actual divergencies can only lead to a postponement of action. In the present case, this truth was to be demonstrated by the fate of the London Conference.

As a consolation to the paper-standard countries the Commission offered some benevolent recognition of their 'difficulties' and admitted that the time and parity for a return to the gold standard can 'only be determined by the proper authorities in each country separately'. In practice this compliance would work out as an undetermined prolongation of the existing dual system of currencies, in which stability was understood by one group as constancy of gold parities and by the opposite group as constancy of the general price-level. But the failure to recognize this contrast prevented the two parties from carrying on useful negotiations establishing workable relations.

On some points the recommendations of the Commission were confused and even contradictory and displayed a reverence for popular delusions which one would not expect to influence an official report of world-wide importance. The Commission rightly uttered a warning against competition in the undervaluation of currencies, but nevertheless recommended that a country returning to the gold standard with deficient reserves should choose a new parity 'consistent with a favourable balance of payments', so that in this way it would be possible 'to attract an adequate reserve without undue effort'. This advice obviously involves the direct recommendation of an undervaluation. As a means for economizing in gold the Commission recommended that bank-notes of small denominations should be replaced by subsidiary coins, and that the use of cheques and clearings should be encouraged—all in order to 'reduce the strain on gold reserves'. Here the idolatry of gold reserves regarded as a 'cover' for the circulation reappears in all its primitive naïvety. The recommendations are of course in themselves quite sound, but they have nothing to do with the need for gold reserves, nor with the basic question of the value of the currency.

The Commission also found time to express some sympathy with the endeavours to raise the price of silver. And, although the crudest forms of silver subventions were rejected, the Commission did not reveal the fundamental fallacy in the gospel propagated by the silver interests, i.e. that silver-using countries, such as China, would benefit by a rise in the price of silver and that the reconstruction of the world's monetary system was to some extent dependent upon a 'rehabilitation of silver'. At the London

Conference the weakness of the Preparatory Commission on this point was exploited by the silver interests, who used the opportunity for organizing an international support of silver with the most disastrous effects (see further, Chapter VII).

V

THE END OF THE GOLD STANDARD

§ 16. *Results of the American Deflation*

DURING the years 1922–8 the United States maintained a remarkable stability in the purchasing-power of the dollar and thereby won a measure of prosperity unparalleled in economic history. In the autumn of 1928 Mr. Hoover was elected President on a programme of furthering the wealth of the nation, and on 4 March 1929 he took office. Seldom has an Administration failed more completely in the fulfilment of its programme than did Mr. Hoover's. He was faced from the very beginning with the troubles caused by the deflationary policy that had been inaugurated in order to combat speculation. When the Stock Exchange broke down in the autumn of 1929 Mr. Hoover sought to save the country by means of his 'Prosperity Propaganda', but having no clear conception of the monetary nature of the depression he was unable to accomplish anything. The deflation went on and the doctrine that the economy of the country had to be adjusted to the lower price-level only served further to force down that level. Eventually it appeared that even debts had to be adjusted to the lower level of prices and creditors were admonished to cut down their claims in proportion to the reduction of the debtors' paying capacity. Thus failures became more and more common and numerous banks had to close, with the consequence that other banks endeavoured to secure for themselves an extraordinary liquidity. But curtailment of credits and selling off of securities could only result in continued deflation and, for the community as a whole, in steadily diminishing liquidity.

All the time economists were sharply criticizing this development and recommending an active monetary policy with the aim of stopping deflation and again raising the general price-level. Such devices, however, were declared to be unsound; they were simply classified as 'inflation', and this shibboleth sufficed to discredit them in public opinion. The deflationists pretended to a better understanding of the conditions necessary for a sound monetary system and even claimed to stand for higher moral principles. This teaching was to prove fatal. Surely, no nation has been more heavily penalized for having followed incompetent counsellors in framing its economic policy. The unprecedented devastation that finally overtook the American economy should stand as a warning to all countries and all times against the teachings of doctrinaire deflationism.

As we have seen above, the Lausanne Conference of 1932, by putting an end to reparation claims, created a singular opportunity for a reversal of the world's monetary policy. Mr. Hoover, however, refused to follow up the Lausanne programme with a general cancellation of War debts, and thereby missed his last opportunity of preventing the threatening catastrophe. When in December 1932 the United States demanded payment of maturing War-debt liabilities the country gave its own economic life a fatal blow. In fact, for years to come America was to lose annually in national income more than a hundred times the annual amount due to her on account of War debts.

The President asked for different compensations, for any concession in respect of these debts. Among such compensations was mentioned more room for American exports. As, however, the United States had led the super-protectionist movement and held the extraordinary position of a creditor country with a large surplus of exports, such a one-sided demand could hardly be of much help in re-establishing equilibrium in the world economy. The President also asked England to return to the gold standard. In the prevailing circumstances this meant that the pound sterling would be tied to the dollar, the mishandling of which had been a main cause of the world crisis. There might have been some reason for demanding that England should join the American money system, if the United States had really possessed a definite and clearly-thought-out monetary policy. Nobody, however, could say that this was the case. In America the most divergent opinions were held as to what were sound monetary principles. The official programme, which was limited to the maintenance of the gold parity, did not deserve to be called a true monetary policy. To maintain a currency in parity with a metal that had shown during the last few years the most violent fluctuations in value could not be a reasonable aim for monetary policy, particularly when it was known that these fluctuations were the result chiefly of measures taken by the country itself in matters of finance, trade, and currency.

Thus, compensations were impracticable and, as long as payment of War debts was insisted upon, nothing could be accomplished in the way of international monetary reconstruction.

The end of the Hoover Administration was marked by extreme depression, dissolution, and hopelessness. Positive action was paralysed by the general election and by that preposterous system that postpones for months the newly elected president's coming into power. It was tragic that an Administration that had started with splendid prosperity should end in such misery—and this in spite of the President's undeniable personal capacity. This experience should serve as a reminder of the necessity for meeting a disorder of a monetary nature with adequate monetary measures. By refusing to do so the United States caused injuries to the international gold-standard system which it was destined not to survive.

In February 1933 I wrote: 'The leading gold-standard countries must understand that it is they themselves that destroy the gold standard by keeping to those ideas by which they have hitherto been guided. . . . Countries that still take an interest in the restoration of the gold standard must understand that their eleventh hour has struck and that further neglect of the most elementary pre-conditions of such a system must be fatal and will probably lead to the abandonment for ever of the aim of constructing an international monetary system on the basis of gold.'[1] The propriety of this warning was demonstrated dramatically when, during the following few weeks, the American banking system broke down and when one of the first measures of the new President had to be the closing of every bank in the country.

§ 17. *America abandons the Gold Standard*

Two days after taking office President Roosevelt, by virtue of the authority invested in the President by a War Emergency Act of 6 October 1917, issued a proclamation ordering for the days 6–9 March 1933 a bank holiday during which all banking transactions should be suspended. This included a prohibition of any transactions in gold or silver coin or

[1] *Manchester Guardian*, 16 February 1933.

bullion. This provisional measure was followed up on 9 March 1933 by a message to Congress asking for the immediate enactment of emergency legislation in banking and currency matters. On the same day Congress, following the receipt of the President's message, passed an Act 'to provide relief in the existing national emergency in banking, and for other purposes'. This Act gave to the President extraordinary powers with regard to the regulation of the currency of the country. The extent of these powers was stated in terms of which the following is the essence:

'During time of war or during any other period of national emergency declared by the President, the President may . . . investigate, regulate, or prohibit . . . any transactions in foreign exchange . . . and export, hoarding, melting, or earmarking of gold or silver coin, or bullion, or currency, by any person within the United States, or any place subject to the jurisdiction thereof.

'Whenever in the judgement of the Secretary of the Treasury such action is necessary to protect the currency system of the United States, the Secretary of the Treasury, in his discretion, may require any or all individuals, partnerships, associations and corporations to pay and deliver to the Treasurer of the United States any or all gold coin, gold bullion, and gold certificates owned by such individuals, partnerships, associations and corporations.'

Punishments for violations were as drastic as those

of the War legislation: fines of up to $10,000, or, in case of a 'natural person', imprisonment for not more than ten years.

On 10 March 1933 the President issued an executive order containing the following monetary provision:

'Until further order, no individual, partnership, association, or corporation, including any banking institution, shall export or otherwise remove or permit to be withdrawn from the United States or any place subject to the jurisdiction thereof any gold coin, gold bullion, or gold certificates, except in accordance with regulations prescribed by or under license issued by the Secretary of the Treasury.'

On 11 March the Secretary of the Treasury issued a statement in which, *inter alia*, the following declarations were made:

'To provide adequate Federal reserve bank currency to satisfy the possible demands under this program, Federal reserve banks are authorized to issue Federal reserve bank notes, not only against Government securities, but also against any member bank note secured by sound assets.

'An executive order forbids all banks to permit withdrawals of currency for hoarding purposes.

'An embargo is imposed upon gold payments, except under license, to prevent gold hoarding. This embargo does not mean that every individual who happens to have one or a number of gold certificates in his roll of currency is to be classified as a hoarder and to be subjected to invidious publicity or other penalty. The provision is aimed at those who continue to retain quantities of gold and thereby hinder the Government's plans for a restoration of public confidence.'

On the following day the President broadcast an address to his people on the banking situation. 'The essential accomplishment of the new legislation', he said, 'is that it makes it possible for banks more readily to convert their assets into cash than was the case before. More liberal provision has been made for banks to borrow on these assets at the reserve banks and more liberal provision has also been made for issuing currency on the security of these good assets. This currency is not fiat currency. It is issued only on adequate security.'

On 8 March the Federal Reserve Board had requested the Federal reserve banks to prepare and forward to the Board 'as complete a list as can be made from information you are able to obtain of the names and addresses of all persons who have withdrawn gold from your bank, or a member bank in your district since February 1, 1933 . . . and authorize them to give publicity to the request'.

On 5 April the President issued an order forbidding the hoarding of gold and requiring all persons to deliver on or before 1 May 1933 all gold coin, gold bullion, and gold certificates now owned by them or coming into their ownership on or before

28 April 1933 (with some exceptions). The drastic punishments in the Act of 9 March were maintained.

On the same day in a press statement the Secretary of the Treasury made some comments on this order and gave the following general motive:

> 'Gold held in private hoards serves no useful purpose under present circumstances. When added to the stock of the Federal reserve banks it serves as a basis for currency and credit. This further strengthening of the banking structure adds to its power of service toward recovery.'

On 12 May 1933 the President approved an Act of Congress dealing primarily with agricultural purchasing-power and farm indebtedness. To this a Title III had been added dealing with monetary matters and giving to the President unlimited powers with regard to the currency of the country. The so-called 'Thomas Amendment' to this Act made all coins and currencies of the United States legal tender for the payment of every debt, public and private. This amendment was equivalent to the cancellation of all obligations to pay in gold coins of a certain standard. The language used in this amendment was, however, rather careless and, in several respects, could give rise to different interpretations.

A knowledge of these somewhat strange and loose methods of monetary legislation is indispensable for judging the possibilities of an international monetary reconstruction, and some extracts from the Act in question will be given here. The first paragraph of section 43 reads as follows:

'Whenever the President finds, upon investigation, that (1) the foreign commerce of the United States is adversely affected by reason of the depreciation in the value of the currency of any other government or governments in relation to the present standard value of gold, or (2) action under this section is necessary in order to regulate and maintain the parity of currency issues of the United States, or (3) an economic emergency requires an expansion of credit, or (4) an expansion of credit is necessary to secure by international agreement a stabilization at proper levels of the currencies of various governments, the President is authorized, in his discretion . . .'

Thereupon some powers are given with regard to the regulation of the currency and the issue of notes, and it was to this paragraph that the Thomas Amendment was added.

The Act continues with the following paragraph:

'By proclamation to fix the weight of the gold dollar in grains nine tenths fine and also to fix the weight of the silver dollar in grains nine tenths fine at a definite fixed ratio in relation to the gold dollar at such amounts as he finds necessary from his investigations to stabilize domestic prices or to protect the foreign commerce against the adverse effect of depreciated foreign currencies. . . . such gold dollar, the weight of which is so fixed, shall be the standard unit of value . . . but in no event shall the weight of the gold dollar be fixed so as to reduce its present weight by more than 50 per centum.'

On 26 May there was introduced in the two Houses of Congress a resolution authorizing the issuance of United States' Government obligations payable in legal tender money rather than in gold and declaring that all debts, public and private, whether they contain the so-called gold clause or not, can be satisfied by payment in legal tender money. This resolution was supported by the Administration. The report of the Committee on Banking and Currency of the House of Representatives contained the following paragraphs:

'1. The occasion for the declaration in the resolution that the gold clauses are contrary to public policy arises out of the experiences of the present emergency. These gold clauses render ineffective the power of the Government to create a currency and determine the value thereof. If the gold clause applied to a very limited number of contracts and security issues, it would be a matter of no particular consequence, but in this country virtually all obligations, almost as a matter of routine, contain the gold clause. In the light of this situation two phenomena which have developed during the present emergency make the enforcement of the gold clauses incompatible with the public interest. The first is the tendency which has developed internally to hoard gold; the second is the tendency for capital to leave the country. Under these circumstances no currency system, whether based upon gold or upon any other foundation, can meet the requirements of a situation in which many billions of dollars of securities are expressed in a particular form of the circulating medium, particularly when it is the medium upon which the entire credit and currency structure rests.

'2. There can be no substantial question as to the constitutional power of the Congress to make this legislation applicable to all obligations, public and private, both past and future. The power of Congress to issue a currency and determine the value thereof and to provide for the borrowing of funds by the Government is express and undoubted. It is also undoubted that Congress has all powers necessary to make the exercise of these two express powers effective. Contracts of private individuals, past or future, are valid and enforceable only in so far as they do not conflict with public policy as enunciated by Congress in the exercise of its constitutional powers. When, therefore, as is declared in this resolution, the enforcement or making of gold-clause provisions obstructs the proper exercise of the congressional powers, such provisions must yield. Nor does the fact that outstanding obligations of the Government are expressed as payable in gold coin impose a limitation, under the circumstances obtaining, upon the exercise of the powers conferred by the Constitution. The Government cannot, by contract or otherwise, divest itself of its sovereign power. All contracts of the Government are made in the light of this inalienable power to legislate as the public interest may demand. It is too well settled to admit of controversy that contracts or provisions of contracts even though not inconsistent with public policy when made, may subsequently become contrary to public policy, as authoritatively announced by the legislative branch of the Government, and that, in such event, they become invalid and unenforceable.'

The Committee was, however, not unanimous in these views. After having recalled the promise given in 1869 in the words: 'The faith of the United States is solemnly pledged to the payment in coin . . . of all the obligations of the United States', the Minority Report said:

'Yet we are now asked to declare that because such provisions "obstruct the power of the Congress to regulate the value of money of the United States", the faith that we solemnly pledged 64 years ago is to be repudiated. What emergency can justify breaking the solemn pledge of a nation? Do "solemn" and "pledge" mean nothing?'

Further:

'The good faith of a nation is its greatest asset. We have boasted that in this no nation is our superior. Upon it we have relied in our international relations. On the very eve of a conference that bids fair to be of supreme consequence to the welfare of the world, we are asked to replace good faith with bad faith, to tell those with whom we confer that whatever agreements we make may be repudiated next day or next year. If we break solemn pledges to our own, what may be expected of those to others?

'We are asking sundry nations to pay us what they owe. Will they be more likely to make good their promises if we set them the example of repudiation?

'That is the right name for it, repudiation, and this bill

ought to be known throughout history as the repudiation bill of 1933.'

The report closed with the words: 'The sanctity of contracts is the cornerstone of our civilization. To violate that sanctity is to invite ruin.'

However, the resolution was passed by both Houses and was approved by the President on 5 June. This remarkable resolution begins with the following declaration:

'Whereas the holding of or dealing in gold affect the public interest, and are therefore subject to proper regulation and restriction; and

'Whereas the existing emergency has disclosed that provisions of obligations which purport to give the obligee a right to require payment in gold or a particular kind of coin or currency of the United States, or in an amount in money of the United States measured thereby, obstruct the power of the Congress to regulate the value of the money of the United States, and are inconsistent with the declared policy of the Congress to maintain at all times the equal power of every dollar, coined or issued by the United States, in the markets and in the payment of debts. Now, therefore, be it *Resolved by the Senate and House of Representatives of the United States of America in Congress assembled*, That (*a*) every provision contained in or made with respect to any obligation which purports to give the obligee a right to require payment in gold or a particular kind of coin or currency, or in an amount in money of the United States measured thereby, is declared to be against public policy;

and no such provision shall be contained in or made with respect to any obligation hereafter incurred. Every obligation, heretofore or hereafter incurred, whether or not any such provision is contained therein or made with respect thereto, shall be discharged upon payment, dollar for dollar, in any coin or currency which at the time of payment is legal tender for public and private debts.'

§ 18. *The Significance of the American Decisions*

Whoever reads the above extracts from the American monetary legislation of 1933 must come to the conclusion that this legislation meant the complete demolition of the gold standard.

The first essential of the gold standard is that gold is recognized as a standard of value to which the value of the currency has continually to adjust itself. This principle has been entirely given up by the American action. It is expressly stated that the President may alter the weight of the gold dollar whenever he finds this necessary in order that certain desiderata should be attained. Among these, special mention is made of the stabilization of domestic prices and the protection of foreign commerce against the adverse effect of depreciated foreign currencies. Thus, stability of the general price-level in terms of dollars, or adjustment of dollar exchanges to some commercial equilibrium parity, are set up as alternative standards for the regulation of the currency of the United States. Clearly, after such statements gold has lost its position as a monetary standard.

The purpose of fixing a gold parity for a country's currency is of course to guarantee the currency against any arbitrary interference on the part of the Administration. The American legislation radically breaks with this principle, giving the President the widest possible power to sever the dollar from any connexion with gold or to choose a new gold parity. The limit of 50 per cent. prescribed for the depreciation of the currency in terms of gold is of only temporary importance. Nobody can doubt that it would be altered should circumstances make it advisable to do so. A new gold parity was subsequently given to the dollar, but this parity is only provisional and its maintenance is dependent upon the discretion of the Administration.

The second essential of the gold-standard system is that the currency is redeemable in gold. Even this principle has been destroyed by the American legislation. The President may at any time suspend the redeemability of the American currency. He can alter the ratio of redemption as he thinks fit and he can prohibit any private monetary possession of gold.

It is often asserted by the friends of the gold standard that it is by far the most popular system, as the public desires to be able at any moment to exchange its currency for 'something tangible'. After the

American declaration there will be no such opportunity. Earlier legislation in other countries has deprived the public of the right to obtain gold coins for its currency but has preserved the right to obtain gold in the form of bullion. The American legislation puts an end even to this right. It is openly proclaimed that the individual has no right at all to get gold. Gold held in private hoards, it is stated, serves no useful purpose. If the President finds that private gold hoarding is contrary to the public interest, private right must yield. Under such circumstances the gold standard will never again offer the public a 'tangible asset'.

The present international discussion about a possible reconstruction of the gold standard is far too formal in its conception of the problem. It is forgotten that the gold standard is essentially a legal order, securing to the individual certain inalienable rights. After what has happened in America there will be no possibility of restoring such a legal order. No new law, however solemnly proclaimed, will be able to restore confidence in the right of the individual to obtain gold for his currency. Everybody will be convinced that any rights asserted will be annihilated as soon as the authorities in power find this to be in the public interest.

Not only may the right of the individual to obtain gold for his currency be at any time cancelled, but he will also find himself classed as an enemy of society if he has made use of his legal rights under the rule of the gold standard to convert some part of his wealth into gold. If the country happens to leave the gold standard he will be ordered, under heavy penalties, to return his gold to the central bank. When in this way private possession of gold comes to be regarded almost as high treason against the community there is certainly no longer any meaning in a 'gold standard'.

The guaranteed redeemability in gold of the currency of a country has never been regarded by orthodox gold-standard theory as solely a private interest. It has primarily been looked upon as the only reliable safeguard for such conduct of the central bank, and, in particular, for such a limitation of the note circulation as will ensure the permanent maintenance of the legal gold parity. The American legislation not only destroyed this safeguard but was framed with the object of making room for an extraordinary extension of the note issue. The legal rules regarding a gold reserve against this issue were set aside and more liberal provisions were made for issuing currency on the security of gold assets, such currency being officially proclaimed not to be 'fiat currency'. This statement seems to remove the idea that the currency must necessarily be secured by a gold reserve of a definite size . This was not done in any clear recognition of the relativity and the conventionality of the need for gold reserves as commonly conceived. Gold reserves were to be revalued and in this way to be increased so as to form an adequate reserve against the inflated currency.

As has been pointed out, the gold standard suffers from the inherent weakness that, in times of distress, a desire for liquidity may arise with a corresponding increase in the demand for gold. In the American case the gold standard was suspended in order to avert such demands. Paper currency was printed to provide the banks with the additional means of payment which they needed in the crisis. This shows how the rush for cash in a crisis will be dealt with in the future: everybody will recall the precedent given in 1933 and expect a suspension of the gold standard.

Now it may, of course, be said, that all this concerns only the United States and need not necessarily prejudice a normal working of the gold standard in other countries. The fact is, however, that every country in the world has treated the gold standard in a similar manner as soon as it has found itself in a so-called emergency situation. The significance of the American experience lies in the radical way in which the monetary system was revolutionized and the whole legal order of the gold standard wrecked. It will never be forgotten how the obligations to pay in gold were treated with a complete disregard of all property rights. To proclaim, as in the resolution of 5 June, that rights to demand payment in gold 'obstruct the power of the Congress' and 'are inconsistent with the declared policy of the Congress', and that therefore every obligation shall be discharged upon payment dollar for dollar in legal tender, expresses an unusual disregard for private property. If the gold standard promotes such violations of the fundamental legal order of society it must certainly be classified as a dangerous piece of machinery.

America's abandonment of the gold standard was in several respects a new experience. Other countries had been forced off gold by deficits in their international balance of payments and by shortness of gold funds. No such forces compelled the United States to abandon the gold standard. The balance of payment had for a decade been in favour of the United States, giving opportunity for an export of capital of large dimensions. True, the surplus on current account has been falling for some years. In 1932, however, it was still 130 million dollars. For the first quarter of 1933 the indications were that the current account was practically in balance and that the losses of gold that had occurred were due exclusively to capital movements. During 1932 the United States had a surplus export of merchandise of about 250 million dollars. In addition, the country received about double that sum in interest and dividends. In January 1933 the gold reserves of the United States had reached the enormous sum of 4,074 million dollars, which was more than a third of the world's total and far surpassed the gold reserve of any other country. If such a gold reserve is deemed insufficient for the maintenance of the gold standard no international gold-standard system will ever be possible. The futility of the orthodox doctrine that gold reserves would guarantee the maintenance of the gold standard was demonstrated in the most striking manner by America's abandonment of the gold standard in 1933.

In the American case the divorce from gold was a deliberate step taken in order to stop deflation and make room for a rise of the general price-level, and also with the object of restoring America's power of competition in the world market. This policy means a break with the sovereign rule of an established gold standard and the setting up of other standards for the management of money.

It is curious to observe how long it took the world to recognize that this was the true implication of America's departure from gold, and how incomplete this recognition has remained even up to the present day.

In the first moment people, even in America, were reluctant to acknowledge that the gold standard had been abandoned. As late as in its letter of April 1933 the National City Bank of New York could write:

'The restriction of gold payments, which was a by-product of the crisis, does not signify the abandonment of the gold standard, but is a measure to maintain the gold holdings of the country against panicky demands. The nature of the legislation shows this, since there is no change in the gold standard act or other monetary laws; and the power given to the President is specifically restricted to "a period of national emergency".'

In the May number, however, the Bank had changed its view and made the following significant and elucidating statement:

'The order of President Roosevelt on April 20 prohibiting until further notice exports of gold from the United States, or earmarkings for foreign account, marks a momentous change of national policy, and signifies a turn to inflationary methods in the effort to find a way out of the depression. Coming at a time when the country's gold holdings are close to record figures, and when its receipts on international account exceed its payments except as flight of capital may temporarily reverse the balance, this action is in no way comparable to the unwilling abandonment of the gold standard by countries having a continuously unfavourable balance of payments. On the contrary, it is everywhere interpreted as a deliberate stroke of policy, and as but one part of a broad program to raise prices.'

In Europe, however, people in leading positions

continued for a long time to look upon the American step as a temporary measure without fundamental importance. It may suffice to quote here the statement on the subject made by Mr. Chamberlain in the House of Commons as late as on 10 July 1933:

'The depreciation of the dollar has undoubtedly brought into operation a very disturbing factor, but one must remember that that depreciation is to a very large extent an unnatural and artificial phenomenon. It is not built upon intrinsic economic and financial factors. It is chiefly the result of speculation, which began in Continental circles, and which has been followed up by American speculation, too, and in the opinion of a good many competent experts the conditions and the facts are such that it is quite possible that we may see a reversal of this process in the autumn when the various factors begin to work in the opposite direction.'

This misjudgement of the situation explains much of the fruitlessness of the endeavours made at that time to arrive at an international agreement on monetary reconstruction. The reference to that much-cherished scapegoat, the speculator, deserves to be noted as a typical sign of weakness in the political argumentation of economic matters.

VI

THE LONDON CONFERENCE

§ 19. *American Preludes*

ENDEAVOURS to reconstruct an international monetary system after the break-down of the gold standard in September 1931 could have had a reasonable hope of success only if an understanding were reached between the two leading powers of the world economy, England and the United States. In May 1932 the British Government sounded the Government of the United States as to their views on a proposal for an economic conference. The answer was favourable, with the reservation that War debts should not be included in the discussions. Action had, however, to be postponed as the summer was occupied by the Lausanne Conference; and when the autumn set in it was found that the American elections made a further postponement necessary. According to the monthly letter of the National City Bank (June 1933), the American Government 'continued to lend its sympathy to the venture, and in October 1932 appointed two distinguished American economists to serve as representatives from this country' on the Preparatory Commission of Experts.

Clearly, effective co-operation between the two countries was impossible so long as America remained on the gold standard and sought her salvation in a continued deflation, whereas, in England, economic life adjusted itself more and more to a sterling standard with constant purchasing-power. In fact, after the first quarter of 1932 the British price-level remained practically constant at the level that had been reached when the gold standard was abandoned. From August 1931 to March 1933 the American price-level (Bureau of Labor) had fallen from 72 to 60. In spite of this serious deflation America felt herself at a disadvantage in competition with British production, which was believed to gain an artificial support from what, from the American point of view, was a continuous depreciation of sterling, the pound-dollar rate having fallen from the old gold parity of 4·87 to 3·28 in December 1932.

The outlook for fruitful co-operation was radically changed from the moment the United States abandoned the gold standard and set up the raising of the price-level and the subsequent stabilization of it as the principal aim of her monetary policy. From that time the monetary programmes of both countries were on such parallel lines that close co-operation seemed only to require agreement on technical points.

The vital importance of such co-operation could not escape President Roosevelt, and he invited the British Prime Minister to visit Washington for a preliminary discussion of the matters that were to come before the London Conference. For the sake of impartiality it was thought desirable to invite representatives of a number of other Governments to similar discussions. Officially all these discussions were reported to have proceeded most harmoniously. Such reports, however, were only possible because the official statements evaded the more controversial points and used general phrases that either meant nothing or were ambiguous. We have seen how fatal such endeavours to reach international agreement had been for the work of the Preparatory Commission. Indeed, the method suffers from a lack of sincerity and candour. It may be possible for some time to veil the real divergences and to give the world the impression that the opposing views have approached one another in a very encouraging manner. But sooner or later the truth will out, with the consequence of a complete break-down of negotiations. The London Conference was to be an outstanding example of the dangers of such a process.

Mr. MacDonald arrived in the United States on 21 April. On the Atlantic the news reached him that the United States had gone off the gold standard, and it was reported that a 'little strain was evident at first as a result of this occurrence'.[1] As a matter of fact, the United States had already abandoned the gold standard by the declarations of 6 and 9 March, and

[1] *Financial Chronicle*, 29 April 1933.

with a little more sense of reality the British authorities would have had time to make themselves familiar with this situation and its consequences. Although the purpose of the subsequent discussions was to come to more concrete and definite proposals than those contained in the report of the Preparatory Commission, it was evidently impossible to accomplish much in that direction. The daily communications issued from Washington sought an exculpation by emphasizing that 'it has never been the purpose of the present discussions to conclude definite agreements'. At the end of the visit, however, the President and the Prime Minister issued a joint statement on the result of their conversations which 'showed that our two Governments were looking with a like purpose and a close similarity of method at the main objectives of the conference . . .'.

'The practical measures which are required for their realizations were analyzed and explored. The necessity for an increase in the general level of commodity prices was recognized as primary and fundamental.

'To this end simultaneous action needs to be taken both in the economic and in the monetary field. Commercial policies have to be set to a new orientation. There should be a constructive effort to moderate the network of restrictions of all sorts by which commerce is at present hampered, such as excessive tariffs, quotas, exchange restrictions, &c.

'Central banks should by concerted action provide an

adequate expansion of credit and every means should be used to get the credit thus created into circulation.

'Enterprise must be stimulated by creating conditions favourable to business recovery and governments can contribute by the development of appropriate programs of capital expenditure. The ultimate re-establishment of equilibrium in the international exchanges should also be contemplated.

'We must, when circumstances permit, re-establish an international monetary standard which will operate successfully without depressing prices and avoid the repetition of the mistakes which have produced such disastrous results in the past.'

From this communication, which undeniably marks a substantial measure of progress, it is clear that the raising of commodity prices was recognized as primary and fundamental. The ultimate establishment of equilibrium in the international exchanges was to be 'contemplated', and the restoration of an international monetary standard was spoken of as a problem of the future.

The conversations which the President had with the representative of France, M. Herriot, ended in a joint statement of a very loose character. 'At no time', the text runs, 'has understanding been more necessary between France and the United States for the maintenance of peace, for progressive and simultaneous economic disarmament and the restoration of stable monetary conditions in an atmosphere of general security.'

The corresponding statement with regard to the Italian discussions was more detailed, but divergences of views were concealed in its confused and ambiguous language.

§ 20. *The Fundamental Cleavage*

Thus it must have been clear long before the London Conference that with regard to the world's monetary question there were two irreconcilable viewpoints. The paper-standard countries wanted a rise of their general price-levels and their subsequent stabilization, and regarded stabilization of exchanges as feasible only when this adjustment of price-levels had proceeded so far as to make it possible to establish certain equilibrium rates; an eventual return to the gold standard was looked upon as the final stage of such a development. The gold countries, on the other hand, insisted upon an immediate return to the gold standard with at least a provisional fixation of gold parities.

These two standpoints were entirely opposed to one another. A fixation of new gold parities with any approximation to the actual purchasing-power of the currencies would compel the paper-standard countries to abandon their price-raising policy. Moreover, such a fixation would expose these countries to all the evil influences that they had tried to escape by leaving the gold standard. The standpoint of the paper-standard countries was by far the more liberal. They wanted to regulate their currencies in the way that they thought would be to their own interest; and left it to the gold countries to do what seemed most suitable to them. The gold countries were not satisfied with remaining themselves on a gold basis but demanded that all other countries should submit to their rule. During the Conference this demand took a more and more dictatorial form, and the gold countries finally refused to take part in any monetary discussion if their terms were not accepted. It was this imperative attitude that at last wrecked the Conference.

It is indeed incredible that it should ever have been thought possible to conceal such a fundamental cleavage of opinions throughout a great international meeting. But the London Conference was held under the auspices of that sort of statesmanship which strives to escape awkward problems by elaborating formulas so vague and so non-committal that everybody may be able to subscribe to them.

At the beginning of the Conference, Mr. Chamberlain drew up on behalf of the British Delegation a monetary programme which in its clearness and definiteness was something of a surprise to the Conference. After some introductory remarks the Chancellor proceeded to state:

'The first proposition which I should like to submit to you is that it is essential to bring about a recovery in the world level of wholesale commodity prices sufficient to yield an economic return to the producers of primary commodities and to restore equilibrium between costs and prices of production generally.' It is clear that the present lack of equilibrium between prices and costs can only be remedied *either* by a further drastic reduction of wages and other costs and by widespread bankruptcies, *or* by a sufficient recovery in the level of wholesale prices.

'In the opinion of the United Kingdom Delegation, an attempt to obtain equilibrium by further large reductions of cost would be attended by intolerable suffering and holds out no hope of success. No doubt it would be possible to restore equilibrium between prices and costs by reducing costs if only prices would remain steady. Under present conditions that does not happen, but, on the contrary, an all-round reduction in costs produces further deflationary effects on prices, so that costs and prices chase one another downwards without ever getting to equilibrium. Moreover, there is one all-important entity in each country which finds it particularly difficult to reduce its own costs; I mean the Central Government. Every Finance Minister in the world knows only too well how tremendously resistant public expenditure is to reduction, if only for the reason that so many of its obligations are fixed in terms of money. A policy of reducing costs and prices has the inevitable effect of very greatly reducing the national income, with the consequence that, in order to balance its accounts, the Government must take by taxation a larger and larger proportion of the income of the country. Sooner or later, usually sooner, this process is found to be intolerable, and countries bent on securing heavy reductions in costs and prices find that they have merely secured an unbalanced Budget for which no practical cure can be found. In the view of the British Delegation, therefore, a solution of our present difficulties must be found by means of a recovery in the price level.

'The fundamental monetary condition of the recovery of prices is that credit should be made available by a policy of cheap money and that such credit should be actively employed. This, together with the revival of business confidence, must form the indispensable background of trade recovery.

'The control of monetary policy is largely in the hands of the Central Banks and the practical steps to give effect to the requisite monetary policy have to be taken by them, and in particular by those of the most important financial centres. These Central Banks should therefore undertake to cooperate with a view to securing the monetary conditions required for a rise in prices. In order that their action may have the desired effect, it is necessary that the policy of cheap and plentiful money should be clearly announced and vigorously pursued. Particularly, the wider extension of what is known as "open market operations" by Central Banks should, in our view, be developed.

'Experience in recent months has shewn that cheap money in itself may not be enough to achieve the desired end rapidly unless means are taken to ensure that the credit made available is actively employed. This in turn depends upon the establishment of a sense of security and confidence in the public, and so again it is seen how inextricably finance and politics are intermingled.

'The question whether Governments can effectively assist in this matter by schemes of Government capital expenditure will also require consideration.'

This excellent statement, which so forcibly expounded the disastrous effects of the deflation policy and gave to the monetary measures their due primary place in the work of reconstruction, obviously corresponded so closely to the policy of the United States that a co-ordination of the monetary programmes of the two leading countries in the world's trade seemed to be within reach. Here, indeed, the London Conference had a singular opportunity for a very important achievement.

As a member of the Conference I suggested that the British programme should be taken as a basis for the discussions of the Conference instead of the report of the Preparatory Commission, which was not only vague and contradictory, but, after America's abandonment of the gold standard, entirely out of date. This idea won much sympathy from representatives of the British Empire, who found it opportune that such a proposal should come from Sweden, so that the appearance of any pressure on the Conference on the part of the British Empire would be avoided. My suggestion was formally proposed to the Conference by the leader of the Swedish Delegation, but the gold countries opposed it, declaring that they had come to the Conference under the condition that the report of the Preparatory Commission should be the basis of the deliberations and that they refused to accept any other conditions.

The Conference never succeeded in surmounting this fundamental cleavage of views.

However, already on 19 June the British Delegation presented a concentrated and definite 'draft resolution' which in three short points expounded the aim and the policy of monetary expansion and the means for realizing it.

I made every effort to bring public opinion to realize the paramount importance at that moment of a co-ordination of British and American monetary policy. On the night between the 18th and 19th of June I delivered from London a broadcast address to the American nation. The following extracts give the essence of this address:

'The new American Administration has from the beginning taken steps for bringing about such a rise in commodity prices, and already with some success. In connection with this policy America has abandoned the gold standard, and there is no prospect of a restoration of the gold standard in the near future. The gold question has for the moment come entirely into the background. The only matter of immediate and urgent importance is the raising of the price level. This is at present the essential interest of the American people, the interest that must dominate its monetary policy.'

'A great country like the United States is no doubt able

to carry through such a programme of monetary expansion alone, but it would be infinitely easier to attain a good result if co-operation could be secured with the other leading country in the world's trade—Great Britain. *First of all* such co-operation would create *confidence*. If Great Britain and the United States were to draw up a common programme for a simultaneous rise of their general price levels, and if they agreed in advance as to the limits of this process, their monetary policy would obviously command a much greater trust in both countries than would be possible if either of them acted alone.'

'*Further*, a proportionate rise of the price levels in these countries would provide a reliable foundation for stabilizing the exchange rate between them. This is in fact the only way of securing lasting stability of the pound-dollar exchange. Some people want to have this exchange stabilized without any agreement between the two countries regarding their monetary policy. In the last few days there has been much talk about an agreement aiming at the stabilization of the pound-dollar exchange, and even definite figures for the stabilized rate have been mentioned. It is, however, obviously impossible to attain any such stabilization until the countries have reached an agreement as to the main lines of their monetary policy.'

'The rate of exchange between two countries is fundamentally determined by the relation between the purchasing power of the different currencies in terms of commodities. If both countries keep their price levels constant there will be no difficulty in maintaining a stable exchange between them. Again, if both countries undertake to raise their price levels proportionally and simultaneously, the rate of exchange between their currencies may also be maintained unaltered. But there can be no question of stability of the rate of exchange if the two countries follow entirely different lines in their regulation of the internal value of their currencies.'

After the statement that had been made on behalf of the British Delegation at the Conference

'there should be no difficulty in securing agreement between the United States and Great Britain as to the main objectives of their monetary policy. Both countries are now practically united in their desire to raise commodity prices, and they should be able to co-operate in suitable efforts to bring about such a rise as they find indispensable in the interest of their national economy and of their mutual trade.'

'Gradually it should be possible to ascertain with sufficient accuracy what rate of exchange between the pound and the dollar would correspond to the relative purchasing power of the two currencies, and therefore be most suitable for maintaining equilibrium in the economic relations of the two countries.'

The present 'singularly good opportunity should be used, and used immediately. It is never good to postpone acting in the belief that you have plenty of time. Here the world's two leading nations can accomplish a great thing to-day. Why should they wait? Immediate action is the more important as it would give that lead that so many smaller nations eagerly expect to get from a concerted British-American monetary policy'.

'Thus a practical stabilization of exchanges would be possible over a wide area, and this stabilization would not be artificial but founded on a common and well considered monetary policy. It would stand every country in the world open to join such a system. No country would need to feel itself excluded. Such a world-wide co-operation for immediate improvement in the economic conditions of mankind ought to be particularly attractive to the American mind.'[1]

As there had proved to be much confusion in the Conference about such conceptions as 'stabilization' and 'depreciation', and as grave misunderstandings had been caused thereby, I presented to the Conference on 20 June a condensed 'Memorandum on Stabilization', in which I emphasized that these terms should never be used without stating in reference to what the value of a currency was assumed to be stabilized or altered. I also showed that exchange stabilization must be classified as a secondary measure which can be successfully contemplated only after general agreement as to the regulation of internal price-levels. Endeavours should always be directed towards maintaining exchanges at equilibrium levels, and no undervaluation should be aimed at. Retaliatory custom duties against a country with a 'depreciated currency' should be condemned as unfair if the currency is not undervalued.

[1] In the *Listener* (5 July) I published a more elaborate article on the subject.

§ 21. *The Collapse of the Conference*

People have often wondered why the London Conference failed so completely as it did. It has been contended that the Conference was too big and that the presence of representatives from so many small States hindered efficient work. There is no truth whatever in this explanation. The Great Powers entirely dominated the Conference but failed to come to an agreement even on the very nature of the problem they had to handle. Moreover, the Conference was crippled by an arrangement which took the principal subject of its deliberations out of its hands. From the beginning conversations upon proposals to stabilize the dollar and the pound sterling in relation to each other and to the franc were begun among representatives of the Treasuries and Central Banks of the United States, Great Britain, and France. Interest was so much concentrated on this discussion that the Conference had practically nothing to do but to wait the decisions of this parallel conference of bankers.

It is a long way from South Kensington to the Bank of England. In the Conference there was doubtless much support for the monetary policy whose principal aim was to raise the general price-level. The Bank, on the other hand, was probably the most energetic advocate of a prompt return to the gold standard. The Governor is not a man who is accustomed to make his opinion known to the public, and the negotiations of the bankers were kept secret. The Bank for International Settlements in Basle, however, had constantly urged a return to the gold standard as the first step to be taken in monetary reconstruction. In its annual report submitted on 8 May 1933 the Board had repeated its 'gold resolution', 'unanimously adopted' in the previous year, and endorsed the views both of the majority of the Gold Delegation and of the Preparatory Commission. At the World Conference, the Board asserted, 'the great desideratum is the general restoration of a reformed gold standard without further delay'. A view unanimously expressed by the Basle Board must obviously represent the opinion of the Governor of the Bank of England. Certainly everything that became known proved that the bankers' conference had urged an immediate, though possibly provisional, stabilization of the gold standard.

Half-way between South Kensington and the Bank is the Treasury. The Chancellor of the Exchequer had, as head of the British Delegation, presented a very sound programme to the Conference. This programme was probably in the main an exposition of the views of the Treasury experts. The Chancellor himself did little to win for his programme the respect it deserved.

The bankers' conference worked out a provisional plan for stabilization in terms of gold and transmitted it to the respective Governments (22 June). The President of the United States naturally found himself unable to accept any such proposal and answered that 'the American Government feels that its efforts to raise prices are the most important contribution it can make and that anything that would interfere with those efforts and possibly cause a violent price recession would harm the Conference more than the lack of an immediate agreement for temporary stabilization'.

It seems that this answer was clear enough, but nevertheless a new programme was transmitted, in which once more, in conformity with unhappy traditions, the terms had been kept so general and noncommittal as to bridge over all divergencies. The countries on the gold standard were to assert their intention of maintaining 'the free working of that standard at current gold parities'. The countries not on the gold standard were to state that they intended ultimately 'to bring back an international standard based on gold under proper conditions', and to agree to take effective measures 'to limit exchange speculation'.

President Roosevelt merits unreserved praise for the directness of his comments on this resolution. His answer, which was received in London on 5 July, was very outspoken indeed, as will be seen from the following extracts:

'I would regard it as a catastrophe amounting to a world tragedy if the great Conference of nations, called to bring about a more real and permanent financial stability and a greater prosperity to the masses of all nations, should, in advance of any serious effort to consider these broader problems, allow itself to be diverted by the proposals of a purely artificial and temporary experiment affecting the monetary exchange of a few nations only. Such action, such diversion, shows a singular lack of proportion and a failure to remember the larger purposes for which the Economic Conference originally was called together.'

'The world will not long be lulled by the specious fallacy of achieving a temporary and probably an artificial stability in foreign exchange on the part of a few large countries only.'

'Old fetishes of so-called international bankers are being replaced by efforts to plan national currencies with the objective of giving to those currencies a continuing purchasing power which does not greatly vary in terms of the commodities and need of modern civilization. Let me be frank in saying that the United States seeks the kind of a dollar which a generation hence will have the same purchasing and debt-paying power as the dollar value we hope to attain in the near future. That objective means more to the good of other nations than a fixed ratio for a month or two in terms of the pound or franc.'

'The Conference was called to better and perhaps to cure fundamental economic ills. It must not be diverted from that effort.'

It cannot be denied, however, that the President treated the Conference rather inconsiderately. He had sent over a Delegation which did not represent his views, and he kept the whole Conference waiting for weeks while he was picking out a head of his 'Brain Trust' and sending him to London. The representatives of the whole world were kept idle in breathless expectation of the arrival of the chief American brain, Professor Mooly, who, when he at last arrived in London, was unable to accomplish anything.

But it is hardly just to blame the President for having altered his ideas since the preliminary conversations in Washington. True, he had not a clearly worked-out programme from the beginning; his language had sometimes been vague and perhaps betrayed some confusion in its conceptions. Yet he had seen the main lines of the problem far more distinctly than the majority of the delegates in London. In a leading article on 5 July *The Times* offered a well-balanced judgement on the controversy between the President and the Conference:

'No doubt it is true that the episode has accentuated the divergence between the views on currency of the Americans on the one hand and of the French and the other gold-standard countries on the other. But that divergence was perfectly well known long before the Conference. Mr. Roosevelt regards a rise in prices as the "primary and fundamental" need and is doing everything in his power to raise the price level in the United States. It is clear that he cannot even contemplate the stabilization of American currency in terms of the currencies of countries in which the price level is stationary or falling.'

The French opinion was that the President had ruined the Conference by his rough message, and the gold-standard countries declared in the Conference that it was impossible for them henceforth to take part in any discussion on monetary questions. The delegates who supported the price-raising policy said that they would feel it intolerable that they should return home without making every effort to bring about that rise in the general level of commodity prices which, in their view, was the primary and fundamental purpose of the Conference. 'If the gold standard countries persist that, as things now are, they cannot even discuss monetary questions, then it remains for the other countries to consider whether they cannot usefully discuss among themselves the measures needed to restore trade and to raise prices in the currencies no longer tied to gold.' (*The Times*, 10 July.)

In consequence of this insuperable cleavage the London Conference collapsed. But, in order to avoid the appearance of failure, the Conference was not closed but only 'adjourned', and stands 'adjourned' to this very day.

§ 22. *The Formation of Monetary Blocs*

In a Committee of the Conference I proposed (June 27):

'that those countries that adhered to the idea of a monetary expansion in order to raise the general level of commodity prices should draw up a common programme for such a policy. Countries opposed to that idea and aiming at an immediate stabilization in terms of gold should draw up a separate programme representing their common view. No attempt should be made to find a general formula covering both views and endeavouring to conceal the fundamental differences of the position of the different countries with regard to the monetary problem.'

It is difficult to understand why the Conference was unable—when at work—to accept such a natural suggestion. And yet, at the end, the only important result to which the Conference led in monetary matters was a clear statement of the different standpoints.

After the refusal of the gold-standard countries to take part in further monetary discussions in London, a meeting of the representatives of the Central Banks of the six chief gold-standard countries signatory to the declaration made at the London Conference—namely, France, Belgium, Holland, Switzerland, Italy, and Poland—was held at the Bank of France on 8 July 'for the purpose of co-ordinating the efforts of the banks for the protection of the exchanges and currencies of these countries'. An official statement was afterwards issued to the effect that the conversations had resulted in complete agreement on the means for giving the fullest practical effect to the declarations of the respective Governments in favour of maintaining in its entirety the gold standard at the present rate of parity; and that the central banks of the countries represented would immediately apply the technical steps the nature of which had been decided upon during the meeting.

By this resolution was created what was later to become known as the 'Gold Bloc'.

The only possibility then left to the other countries was to form a bloc of their own. The British Dominions eagerly insisted upon a common declaration of the British Empire on monetary policy. Considerable difficulties had to be overcome, however, before unanimity on such a declaration could be secured. Again there was manifest a certain reluctance on the part of the Chancellor of the Exchequer to side with the policy of monetary expansion and to dissociate himself from dependence upon the Gold Bloc. The Dominions, according to the account of *The Times* on 31 July 1933,

'were dissatisfied with Great Britain's management of sterling, feeling that not nearly enough had been done to raise the level of sterling prices, and that far more attention had been given to maintaining stable exchanges with the gold currencies than to the internal needs of the British Empire or even of Great Britain. They more than suspected that the Exchange Equalization Fund was being used to peg the pound to the franc instead of simply to iron out fluctuations due to speculation or merely seasonal causes. They pressed the British Government to give a bolder lead to the sterling countries.'

Thus the positive policy of curing the devastation inherent in prolonged deflation by means of a controlled but substantial monetary expansion had to strive against some resistance, or at least some hesitation, on the part of the Chancellor. Moreover, there was always in the background the impenetrable enigma of what might be the policy of the Bank of England. The Bank represented a power whose willing and sincere co-operation was indispensable. But the monetary ideas prevailing at the Bank were, as we have seen, not very favourable to the policy advocated by the Dominions.

However, after the close of the London Conference a meeting of the United Kingdom Delegation and the representatives of the Dominions issued on 27 July an 'Empire Declaration' which may be regarded as the constitution of what is now known as the 'Sterling Bloc'. It was declared to be of the greatest importance that the rise in prices that had begun should continue. The ultimate level to be aimed at should be such as would restore the normal activity of industry and employment, ensure an economic return to the producer of primary commodities, and harmonize the burden of debts and fixed charges with economic capacity.

'The Governments of the British Commonwealth should persist by all means in their power, whether monetary or economic, within the limits of sound finance in the policy of furthering the rise in wholesale prices until there is evidence that equilibrium has been re-established. . . . Thereupon they should take whatever measures are possible to stabilize the position thus attained.'

'The ultimate aim of monetary policy should be the restoration of a satisfactory international gold standard under which international co-operation would be secured and maintained with a view to avoiding, so far as may be found practicable, undue fluctuations in the purchasing power of gold.'

In the meantime stability of exchange rates between the countries of the Empire should be aimed at and

'aided by the pursuit of a common policy of raising price levels.'

'The adherence of other countries to a policy on similar lines would make possible the attainment and maintenance of exchange stability over a still wider area.'

With these clearly defined objectives the policy of the Sterling Bloc stood out as the only solid rock in a swamp of unsettled controversies and vague aspirations.

VII

SILVER

§ 23. *The Silver Agitation*

AN account of the downfall of the gold standard would be incomplete without at least a brief reference to its effects on the monetary position of silver. During the crisis the shortcomings of the gold standard were exploited by the silver agitation in favour of what was called a 'rehabilitation of silver'. That such a policy is not the way out of the present troubles will be evident from the following record of the principal arguments and the results of the great silver campaign of recent years.

One would have thought that the defeat which the silver agitation suffered at the end of the nineteenth century would have removed once and for all the silver question from the platforms of monetary policy. The arguments brought forward in favour of a 'rehabilitation of silver' had been entirely confuted by economic science and, with the exception of China, practically the whole world had, as it seemed, definitely accepted the gold standard.

In the United States, however, the silver agitation was never quite laid low. It continued to be supported by the silver producers, who in the post-War troubles of the gold standard believed they had found an opportunity for bringing their case once more into the foreground. They won the support of other silver-producing countries, such as Mexico, as well as of some people engaged in Eastern trade and a number of more or less cranky currency reformers. All the rusty arguments of nineteenth-century bimetallism were again taken up and exploited with the utmost recklessness in a renewed world-wide silver agitation. This agitation naturally received a great stimulus when after 1928 the price of silver began to fall violently.[1]

The most important of the arguments used was that the world supply of gold had proved insufficient and must be supplemented by silver in order that the monetary system should be given a sufficiently broad basis. This reasoning seemed convincing enough to the general public, educated to believe in the necessity for a metallic basis of the monetary system and to look upon percentage metallic 'cover' as the true criterion for judging the value of a currency. However, even if it was deemed desirable to keep some

[1] In 1913, the year before the War, silver had commanded an average price in New York of 61 cents. After the War the price had risen considerably in sympathy with the general inflation of commodity prices, but already in 1921 it was brought back to an average price of 63 cents. In 1928 the average was 58 cents, but from that time on the price of silver, in connexion with the general economic crisis, rapidly fell to such an extent that in 1931 a minimum was reached of 26 cents.

metallic reserves, the monetary gold stock of the world was large enough to meet any real need if only the rules of the gold economizing policy had been observed and if, in particular, the *legal* minimum requirements of gold cover had been reduced in accordance with the proposal of the Gold Delegation, or had been entirely abolished, as I suggested. If, some time in the future, the world has to face an insuperable shortness of gold, an addition of silver to the reserves would certainly not be the way out of the difficulty. Once gold is abandoned as a fixed standard of value it will always be possible by a suitable revaluation of gold reserves to make them suffice for any practical purposes; or it may at last be discovered that metallic reserves are no real necessity.

As regards the United States, her stock of gold was large enough to meet all conceivable needs for metallic means of payment, and it was entirely superfluous to increase her monetary reserves by supplementing them with silver. Naturally, this was still more so after the abandonment of the gold standard in 1933 and the subsequent revaluation of the American gold reserves.

The fear of a serious shortage in the supply of gold was increased by the belief that a further fall in the price of silver might drive the silver countries over to the gold standard and that an insatiable demand for gold would then arise. As a matter of fact, this consequence had been avoided when India adopted the gold standard, and there was no reason why China should not follow the example of India. Moreover, China had traditionally a large silver import and would substantially improve her balance of payments if she ceased buying silver. Thus, under normal circumstances, she would have no need for large reserves in order to protect a well-balanced exchange value of her currency. The truth as to the alleged need for an addition of silver to gold reserves was unusually well expounded by the London *Statist* in its number of 14 February 1931, where it was said:

'We do not believe, however, that the cause of silver is in itself great enough to justify the dangerous experiment of bimetallism. The whole tendency to-day is away from the automatic functioning of a metallic standard and towards its conscious and scientific control. The main antithesis to-day is between, on the one hand, reason and intelligence as applied to monetary policy and, on the other, passive subservience to the vagaries of arbitrary changes in the supply of and demand for whatever metal or metals are chosen as the basis of our monetary systems. We are inclined to reject bimetallism because it will draw away attention from this essential choice facing the monetary authorities of the world. If we are suffering from a shortage of gold that shortage can be made good by diminishing the monetary demand for it and especially by lowering the central banks' ratios between gold and sight liabilities. It would not be a constructive step to remedy that shortage by rendering silver eligible for a place in central bank reserves and by basing the whole monetary structure upon two instead of one essentially unstable elements.'

The fall in the price of silver was also used as a direct argument in favour of some form of silver rehabilitation. Naturally, a violent change in economic conditions is always followed by disturbances of a more or less harmful nature, and thus it was not unreasonable that endeavours should be made to stop or mitigate the fall in the price of silver. The importance of this argument was, however, very much exaggerated, and misleading practical conclusions were drawn from it.

In the first place the fall in the price of silver cannot be regarded as an isolated phenomenon. Silver has sunk in value in relation to gold, but this fact might equally well be described as a rise in the value of gold relative to that of silver. A definite statement on this point is possible only if we have agreed upon a certain standard of value.

Taking for comparison the average commodity price-levels of 1928, the year before the great crisis, and denoting them by 100, we find that the London quotation of silver had fallen in the first quarter of 1931 to something like 50. This might seem a very heavy fall indeed, and was in fact represented in the silver agitation as being so. At the same time, however, commodity prices, according to the index number of the *Statist*, had fallen to nearly 70. It follows that, in terms of commodities on the London market, silver had likewise come down to about 70. Thus silver had fallen in terms of commodities by just as much as commodities had fallen in terms of gold, and these two movements combined account for, and are about equally responsible for, the fall of silver in terms of gold.

For the silver-using countries the fall in the price of silver meant an inflation of commodity prices, which may have been attended by some drawbacks, but which was perhaps beneficial on the whole. At any rate, the deflation that the gold countries had to go through was a far more serious evil, and there was certainly no reason for speaking of the sufferings of the silver countries as something especially entitled to call for world attention.

During 1931 and 1932 commodity prices in terms of gold continued to fall heavily and gold countries had to go through a prolonged and harmful process of deflation. As silver declined much less in terms of gold, silver-using countries had to face a similar, though somewhat mitigated, deflation, and that was doubtless for them a serious embarrassment. It was sheer madness, of course, to try to help them by raising the price of silver in terms of gold and thereby forcing the silver countries to a still more violent deflation.

On the whole, much of the interest which the silver agitation displayed for China and other silver-using countries hardly deserves a better name than bluff. Grandiloquent phrases were used to describe the responsibility of the Western World for the catastrophic fall in the price of silver which had halved the savings of the broad masses of China and India, and it was proclaimed that equity and humanitarianism demanded that the gold-standard countries should regard it as their inescapable duty to ensure at least the maintenance of a minimum price for silver. By giving due consideration to the rights and welfare of the East the gold countries would be able to re-establish confidence in the ancient standard of half the world.

It was argued in particular that a rise in the price of silver would increase the purchasing-power of the silver countries and thus benefit both those countries themselves and world trade. This is a fallacy. It is not true that silver countries pay in silver when they buy goods from abroad. On the contrary, they pay by means of an export of commodities which is usually greater than the import and thus gives them a surplus available for the purchase of gold and silver. In the five years ending with 1930 the combined net imports of silver into India and China averaged approximately 200,000,000 ounces per year, out of a total world production of about 255,000,000 ounces.

Under such circumstances the silver countries can derive no advantage from a rise in the price of silver. So long as they desire to buy silver it is hardly in their interest to have to pay an artificially enhanced price for it.

In fact, behind the eloquent benevolence displayed to the East there lay a solid, though not a very enlightened, self-interest. It was contended that the low price of silver gave the silver-using countries an undue advantage in competition on the world market and at the same time worked as a high tariff wall for protecting their home industries. By aid of this argument it was possible to win over to the silver agitation not only great export interests, such as the American cotton-growers and the Lancashire cotton industry, but also producers, including agriculturalists, who were exposed to competition from the East.

In England a lively campaign was waged in support of silver and men otherwise distinguished for their clear judgement were drawn into this agitation. A memorable meeting was held in London in September 1931 under the auspices of the 'China Association', with Sir Robert Horne in the chair. This meeting unanimously stated its conviction 'that the raising of the price of silver and its restoration to a place in the world's monetary system offers the quickest and most effective remedy to the present disastrous fall in prices', and expressed the hope 'that the Governments principally concerned will at the earliest possible moment confer with this object in view'. An international conference on silver was declared to hold out prospects of immediate advantage, reference was made to the unanimous resolution passed in the beginning of the year by the Senate of the United States, and the President was requested to call such a conference. The meeting also constituted a 'Silver Association' to deal with the silver problem.

At that time of general monetary upset it was perhaps natural enough to seek a refuge in such remedies. It is more unpardonable that after three years of discussion and after the successful stabilization of the sterling system, the 'rehabilitation' of silver could continue to be urged as being of primary importance to the world economy. It may be worth while to recall how far the silver agitation went in this respect as late as in August 1934, when a pamphlet on *Silver Money, the Case for its Restoration* was issued with a Foreword by Lord Desborough, Lord Greenway, Lord Hunsdon, Sir Henri Deterding, and Sir Montagu de P. Webb. This pamphlet, which pretended to represent 'the world's most authoritative opinion', is a bewildering muddle of false argumentation. One striking contradiction in the reasoning is noteworthy. On the one hand, the promotion of the well-being of the silver countries by increasing their purchasing-power is given as a reason for raising the price of silver. On the other hand, a low price of silver is represented as furthering the competition of the silver countries on the world market and thus giving them a dangerous advantage which ought to be counteracted by raising the price of silver. Sir Henri Deterding probably comes nearest to the truth when he says:

'When the Western World sold to the Far East large quantities of silver at two or five times the present price in exchange for goods, was it a sound procedure for the Western World afterwards to lower the price of that very same silver previously sold at such a good price?'

Another witness, represented in the pamphlet as a man with a great experience of China's trade, says:

'It is largely through the lowered gold price of silver that China has wakened up to her great industrial potentiality. Given peace in her domain, she will before long swamp European markets with her merchandise.

'Silver cannot be allowed to remain at its present level any longer. Once the East is able to manufacture for its own need, the loss to the Empire will be irreparable.'

During the most violent fall in the price of silver, say in the years 1929 and 1930, some undervaluation of the silver currencies probably took place from which the silver countries derived a temporary trade advantage. Later on, however, endeavours to bring about a substantial rise in the price of silver could not but lead to an overvaluation of the silver currencies, with the consequence that the silver countries would be forced to go through an intolerable deflation and eventually to abandon the silver standard. This consequence ought to have been patent enough to every one with any knowledge of the elements of economic reasoning. And, since England in September 1931 had found it impossible any longer to pursue the deflation enforced by the continual rise in the value of gold, and thus had had to leave the gold standard, it ought to have been evident to the whole business world that the logical course of events could not be different in silver countries. Those politicians and business men who for years after that experience persisted in representing a rise in the price of silver as a particular blessing for the silver countries will perhaps feel somewhat uneasy in face of the actual results of such a silver policy, of which the world is now a most embarrassed witness.

In the United States the prime movers in the silver agitation were, of course, the mining interests, the representatives of which used their political influence most unscrupulously to further their economic advantage. Bills and resolutions in aid of silver were repeatedly brought before Congress, where they found growing support. A fresh argument was added when the country was exposed to the evils of unemployment on an unparalleled scale. Endeavours to combat unemployment had turned economic common sense upside down and afforded some appearance of justification for a violation of the most elementary economic principles. A policy for raising the price of silver might be represented as a suitable means for furthering a great extension of the American mining industry and thus providing work for a great many unemployed. This argument seems to have turned the political scale in favour of the silver interest with the calamitous results which we shall now have to study.

§ 24. *Measures for the Rehabilitation of Silver*

At the London Conference the American silver interests succeeded, under the leadership of Senator Pittman, in securing a 'Silver Agreement' (22 July 1933), according to which the Indian Government consented to restrict its current sales of demonetized silver to an average of 35 million ounces annually during a period of four years commencing 1 January 1934, and China and Spain made concessions of a similar nature. On the other hand, the Governments of the five leading producing countries, the United States, Mexico, Canada, Peru, and Australia, agreed to absorb a total amount of 35 million ounces per annum. The American Government were to take at least 24·4 million ounces a year from the silver produced in the United States. In pursuance of this agreement President Roosevelt issued on 21 December 1933 a proclamation ordering the mints to buy newly mined domestic silver at the mint par of $1·2929 with a deduction of 50 per cent., i.e. at a price of about 64·6 cents. This price was about double the quotations prevailing in New York before the London Conference and thus meant a very substantial premium to the American producers.

After that concession the President, obviously much against his will, was driven step by step into a pronounced silver rehabilitation policy. On 19 June 1934 he signed the famous Silver Purchase Act, which was in reality a compromise between the standpoint of the President and the extreme proposals of the silver men.

In the message to Congress on 22 May 1934, with which the President introduced this legislation, he had made the following statement:

'We can proceed with this program of increasing our store of silver for use as a part of the metallic reserves for our paper currency without seriously disturbing adjustments in world trade. However, because of the great world supply of silver and its use in varying forms by the world's population, concerted action by all nations, or at least a large group of nations, is necessary if a permanent measure of value, including both gold and silver, is eventually to be made a world standard.'

From this it is evident that the President actually aimed at some form of universal bimetallism.

The Act itself declares it 'to be the policy of the United States that the proportion of silver to gold in the monetary stocks of the United States should be increased, with the ultimate objective of having and maintaining one-fourth of the monetary value of such stocks in silver'.

The Treasury was to issue silver certificates at a rate of $1·29 an ounce, which corresponded to the old American ratio of 16 : 1. As, however, the President had by his proclamation on 31 January 1934 reduced the gold content of the dollar, the new mint ratio between the metals was approximately 27 ounces of silver to 1 of gold. The more extreme silver advocates were not satisfied with that ratio but wanted to raise the mint value of silver to the old ratio, which would mean a silver price of about $2·18. For silver situated in the United States on 1 May 1934 the purchase price of the Treasury would not exceed 50 cents a fine ounce. For newly mined domestic silver the price had been fixed, as already mentioned, at 64·6 cents. It was estimated at that time that the carrying out of the programme would require a purchase of 1,600 million ounces of silver, which was, of course, a fantastic figure. Yet nobody could fix any definite limit to the amount of silver to be purchased, as it would be increased in proportion to any further growth in the American gold reserve.

At first this legislation seems to have been regarded

as permissive rather than mandatory. However, silver purchases in 1934 were on a very large scale. On 9 August the President ordered silver holdings in the country (with some exceptions) to be surrendered to the Treasury within 90 days against payment of 50·01 cents per fine ounce. Under this order some 111 million ounces were received during the remainder of the year. In addition the Treasury bought newly mined domestic silver to an amount that has been estimated for the year 1934 at 21·4 million ounces. The purchases on the international markets during the same year are estimated at about 185 million ounces. Thus the Government's total silver acquisitions for the year would amount to 317·4 million ounces.[1]

In April 1935 the President raised the price for home-produced silver by lowering the deduction from the mint price, first to 45 and then to 40 per cent., which meant that the price was raised to approximately 71 and 77½ cents respectively.

Under such circumstances it was no wonder that international speculation began to reckon with the prospect of a rise in the silver price on the international markets as well. The average silver price in London, which for May 1933 had been 19·05 and for May 1934, 19·27 (pence per troy ounce), rose to 33·87 for May 1935. Thereafter the price fell and for November stood at 29·28. In spite of such high prices

[1] Lawrie, *Gold and Silver*, p. 208.

the American Treasury continued its purchases on the international markets on a huge scale.

A most important consequence of this policy was that the silver coinage of China began to be shipped to the United States in great quantities. It is estimated that over 200 million Chinese dollars were exported. Thus China was threatened with the calamity of being deprived of her current money, and gradually resorted to defensive measures, such as a tax and an 'equalization fee' on exports of silver, and foreign exchange control. Moreover, the rising price of silver caused an intolerable overvaluation of the Chinese currency, which forced upon China a very harmful and dangerous process of internal deflation. In the autumn of 1934 the Chinese Government addressed two notes to the United States pointing out that any 'further material silver price increase would cause very serious injury to China, possibly severe panics'; and that China might be forced to consider 'the gradual introduction of a gold basis currency'. As no satisfactory answer was received the Chinese Government in October 1934 raised the silver export duty from $2\frac{1}{4}$ per cent. to 10 per cent. and introduced an equalization fee to offset any differential between the price of silver in London and the rate of exchange as fixed by the Central Bank of China. Thus China had been virtually forced off the silver standard and began to approach the sterling bloc.

In the autumn of 1935 Sir Frederick Leith Ross went to China to discuss the monetary situation with the Nanking Government. The result was that on 3 November that Government issued a currency reform edict, which stipulated that within three months from 4 November all silver must be surrendered to the Government in exchange for bank-notes. The Central Bank was to be reorganized along modern lines and charged with the duty of maintaining a stable exchange value of the Chinese currency. This was to be a paper currency tied to the pound sterling at the fixed rate of exchange of 1*s.* 2½*d.* Thus a substantial devaluation took place, the average quotation for October being 1*s.* 5·56*d.* The new rate was maintained practically unaltered up to the end of the year. So far China may be regarded as having joined the sterling bloc. Unfortunately, the effectiveness of this edict is rather dubious. The Nanking Government is not very firmly established, and will hardly be able to enforce the embargo on silver in outlying districts, especially in North China. The currency situation was further complicated by the protest against the measure raised by Japan, who wanted to sever North China from the rest of the country and disliked seeing the silver reserves of that region surrendered to the Nanking Government. It is deplorable that such political difficulties should stand in the way of a currency reform which seems to have been quite sound in itself. The new parity chosen should give the Chinese currency a margin of safety. At any rate it had the immediate effect of raising commodity prices in Shanghai. Of course, the external silver price very much exceeded the internal price offered by the Nanking Government, and a very strong incentive to smuggling was created. This smuggling naturally weakened the financial position of the Nanking Government, but must, on the other hand, have favourably affected China's balance of payments.

In December 1935 the American Government ceased buying silver in London. Possibly, Mr. Morgenthau only wanted to make himself independent of the London Market or of speculators influencing that market; another version is that he followed a systematic policy of inducing silver countries, particularly Mexico and China, to join a bimetallic dollar system; in that case the further silver operations of the United States must be watched with a large measure of distrust. In any case the immediate result was a sharp fall in the price of silver. On 24 December the spot price at New York reached $49\frac{3}{4}$ cents a fine ounce, which is $15\frac{5}{8}$ cents below the price at the end of November. The London silver price, which in the autumn and up to 6 December had stood somewhat above 29*d.*, after that date suddenly fell, so that on 24 December a rate of $20\frac{7}{8}$*d.* was reached. Later on some improvement took place. A moderate and approximately constant price of silver would doubtless be of great value for stabilizing the currency situation in China. The incalculable silver-buying policy of the United States remains, however, an extremely disturbing element not only to China but to the world at large. The United States cannot hope to increase the stability of the international monetary system by linking it in any way to a metal which is subject, like silver, to such violent fluctuations in value.

The most paradoxical effect of the policy of raising the price of silver appeared in the case of Mexico, which, as the largest silver-producing country in the world, was supposed to be especially favoured by a high price of this metal. Mexico had a silver currency with a stable exchange in relation to the American dollar. At this exchange level, the melting-point of the Mexican peso was approximately 72 cents. When this price was surpassed the Mexican Government called in all outstanding silver pesos and substituted for them a paper money secured by the retired silver coins. Mexico sent representatives to Washington emphasizing the difficulties to which Mexico was exposed by the American silver purchases. The result was that the United States ceased to buy silver at prices higher than 65⅝ cents (24 August 1935). According to later reports Mexico is entering into some sort of currency agreement with the United States on a bimetallic basis.

Although India is on the sterling standard, a heavy rise in the price of silver may cause her serious difficulties. If silver should rise to 48·7*d.* per ounce the silver content of the rupee would be worth its exchange value and India would begin to lose her silver circulation. The country would then also be threatened with an overvaluation of its currency and would thus be put in much the same situation as China is in now. The most natural remedy would probably be to reduce the silver content of the rupee. Other countries with a large silver circulation could be forced to a similar measure by a continued rise in the price of silver.

Thus the American silver-buying policy will have the effect of forcing countries off the silver standard and driving silver out of circulation. This was not precisely the purpose of the policy that proposed to 'support silver' or actually to 'restore silver to its time-honoured place in the world's currency system'.

The American silver producers are already beginning to realize the mistake and to urge that the American Government should limit the price it offers for foreign silver to something between 60 and 65 cents an ounce. On this subject a very illuminating address was delivered before the American Mining Congress at Chicago on 24 September 1935 by Francis H. Brownell, Chairman of the Board of Directors of the American Smelting and Refining

Company. He emphasized the fact that the aim of the Silver Purchase Act was to further rather than to hinder the ultimate use of silver as well as gold in a future monetary system of the world. Congress could not have thought that the Act would be so enforced as to induce other nations to melt their silver currencies and sell the resultant silver to the United States. He calculates that the amount of silver available for purchase by the United States in the following five years, without drawing upon the sources of coined silver or fabricated silver, is something around 1,100 million ounces, which should roughly exhaust the remaining buying capacity under the Silver Purchase Act. He thinks that the United States should not pay more than 65 cents for foreign silver and that 60 cents is a more desirable level at present. He concludes that the silver purchases ought to be extended over the next five years in order to give the world time for the restabilization of its currencies. This stabilization will definitely determine 'the future of both gold and silver, and if the price of silver remains substantially steady and not subject to wide fluctuations, the further probability of greater utilization of silver by other nations will be decidedly enhanced'. The American mining interest is, however, by no means forgotten by Mr. Brownell. He points out that the American Government makes a profit of about 52 cents per ounce by paying the mining industry 77 cents and assigning to the same silver a mint value of $1·29, and he suggests that this profit might suitably be used for combating unemployment by an extension of mining activities. Thus the Government would be fully justified in paying a higher price for home-produced silver!

VIII

THE PRINCIPAL MONETARY SYSTEMS AFTER THE LONDON CONFERENCE

§ 25. *The Dollar*

On 15 January 1934 the President of the United States delivered a message to Congress in which he recommended Congress to fix the upper limit of 'permissible revaluation' of the dollar at 60 per cent. of its old gold value. The lower limit had previously been fixed at 50 per cent. (Act 12 May 1933).

This recommendation was included in the Gold Reserve Act of 1934 signed by the President on 30 January. Thus a close connexion was established between dollar and gold, although the President did not think it desirable 'that an exact value be now fixed'.

On 31 January, however, the President issued a proclamation fixing the weight of the gold dollar at such a level as to correspond to a new gold par of $35 per troy ounce of fine gold (as against the previous price of $20·67). The new par was 59·06 per cent. of the former one. The provisional character of the measure is strongly emphasized in a passage which deviates somewhat from common legislative language: 'Notice is hereby given that I reserve the right by virtue of the authority vested in me to alter or modify this proclamation as the interest of the United States may seem to require.'

As this step has often been falsely interpreted as a break with the President's former monetary policy, it is desirable that the actual purport of the new legislation should be stated in its original terms. The first message is introduced by a reference to 'the progress we are making in restoring a fairer price level and with our purport of arriving eventually at a less variable purchasing power for the dollar'. This seems to prove that the President is still adhering to his aim, proclaimed at the London Conference (§ 21), of seeking 'the kind of dollar which a generation hence will have the same purchasing and debt-paying power as the dollar value we hope to attain in the near future'.

The message also speaks of a future 'world-wide agreement, creating a uniform monetary policy' and mentions the London Silver Agreement as a step in this direction. Thus some form of bimetallism is contemplated, obviously as a means for furthering the President's principal aim, a lowering and subsequent stabilization of the purchasing-power of the dollar. The relative stabilization of the dollar in terms of gold and the establishment of an exchange equalization fund of 2,000 million dollars are represented as steps towards the world-wide agreement. At the same time, however, the message refers to 'the other principal precious metal—silver', which is said to constitute 'a very important part of our own monetary structure' and to be 'a crucial factor in much of the world's international trade'.

At the end of the message the President again emphasizes that 'our national currency must be maintained as a sound currency which, in so far as possible, will have a fairly constant standard of purchasing power and be adequate for the purposes of daily use and the establishment of credit'. Surely such a message cannot be interpreted as an expression for a policy aiming at a restoration of the gold standard.

The proclamation of 31 January was introduced by two paragraphs giving the motives for the revaluation of the dollar. These paragraphs read as follows:

'Whereas, I find, upon investigation, that the foreign commerce of the United States is adversely affected by reason of the depreciation in the value of the currencies of other governments in relation to the present standard value of gold, and that an economic emergency requires an expansion of credit;

'Whereas, I find, from my investigation, that, in order to stabilize domestic prices and to protect the foreign commerce against the adverse effect of depreciated foreign currencies, it is necessary to fix the weight of the gold dollar . . .'

From this quotation it is seen that the revaluation of the dollar was undertaken for two reasons: (1) for meeting the undervaluation of foreign paper currencies; and (2) for an immediate rise and subsequent stabilization of the commodity price-level in the United States. Thus the legislation of January 1934 is essentially in line with the monetary policy which the President had stood for during the London Conference. It should also be observed that the revaluation is entirely provisional and that the President expressly reserves for himself the right to alter it at any moment he thinks fit. Obviously such an alteration will be directed by the two motives here referred to, which have nothing to do with gold as a standard.

The President still has the legal authority to reduce the gold par of the dollar to 50 per cent. of the old par, which is equivalent to $41·34 per fine ounce. A margin between 50 and 60 per cent. of the old par is very large indeed, extending as it does to 20 per cent. of the lower limit. A reduction of the gold par down to 50 per cent. is by no means outside practical politics.

'In the fall of 1934 when there was a lull in employment and industrial activity, efforts were made by the Committee for the Nation and the American Farm Bureau Federation to obtain favourable action by the President in reducing the dollar to 50c., but confronted by large Treasury financing operations, the President took no action.'[1]

Besides, nobody doubts that if the President should

[1] Lawrie, *Gold and Silver*, p. 194.

find the interests of the United States to require a further reduction of the gold par beneath 50 per cent., he would easily get the consent of Congress to such reduction. Thus there can be no talk of the United States having returned to gold as a definite standard of value. And as to the redeemability in gold of the American currency it must be kept in mind that there exists within the States no private property in gold.

In the fourth annual report of the Bank for International Settlements[1] the American Legislation of January 1934 is said 'again to have linked the dollar to gold'. President Roosevelt is reported to have 'revealed how extensively his opinions had evolved since his messages to London'. In support of this somewhat strange interpretation the report selects two pronouncements used as motives for the establishment of the new Exchange Fund and simply leaves out of count all the essential statements that have been quoted above. The first pronouncement reads: 'That we may be further prepared to bring some greater degree of stability to foreign exchange rates in the interests of our people.' The other (from Section 10 *a* of the Gold Reserve Act) reads: 'For the purpose of stabilizing the exchange value of the dollar.' Now everybody knows that the American Exchange Stabilization Fund has much the same

[1] Basle, 14 May 1934.

purpose as the English model; in fact, the motives here quoted might just as well have been used by Mr. Chamberlain. Nobody, however, would contend that the purpose of the British Exchange Equalization Fund is the restoration of an international gold standard. The primary motive for creating the American Fund is doubtless that quoted above: 'to protect the foreign commerce against the adverse effect of depreciated foreign currencies'. The American Fund was established as a counterbalance to the British, and its immediate purpose was clearly that the American authorities should have something to say in regard to such a regulation of the pound-dollar exchange as would most nearly correspond to an economic equilibrium.

Under these circumstances the interpretation given by the Bank for International Settlements is entirely misleading. In fact, it is only a continuation of the old efforts to veil the real divergencies of views on the gold standard. We have seen how disastrous these efforts have been for a sincere international collaboration in monetary reconstruction, and it can only be regretted that such efforts should continue to be made by an authoritative body like the Bank for International Settlements.

At the new par the dollar was undoubtedly undervalued for the time being. One might expect, therefore, that foreign gold would be offered on a large scale in exchange for dollars; and that the balance of payments, usually in favour of America, would tend to become still more so. Reckoned from the previous par the American price of gold had been raised by nearly 70 per cent. As America was willing to pay so much for gold and had the necessary purchasing-power in her surplus balance of payments, gold was bound to go to America.

In fact, the consequence of the revaluation of the dollar was an immense flow of gold into the United States. In terms of new dollars the American gold stock amounted at the end of January 1934 to 6,829 million dollars. At the end of the year it had risen to 8,238 million dollars. This rapid growth continued during 1935, with the result that in December the stupendous figure of 10,000 million dollars was exceeded. Domestic production had contributed to this growth, but it was chiefly the result of net gold imports, which for the period from the revaluation to the end of 1935 amounted to about 2,900 million dollars. Member bank reserve balances, which in January 1934 stood at 2,740 million dollars (average of daily figures), rose to 4,037 million dollars in December the same year, and to 5,789 million dollars on 27 November 1935. 'Excess reserves' had in the latter part of November 1935 exceeded the sum of 3,000 million dollars. There was thus the possibility of a vastly increased supply of means of payment.

The question was how far this possibility was to be used and what would be the effect on the general price-level.

According to the index of the Labor Bureau this level had risen from 60 at the beginning of the Roosevelt Administration to 72 in January 1934, that is to say by 20 per cent. During 1934 the general price-level continued to rise, but at a slower rate. In January 1935 the figure 79 was reached. Thus for these twelve months the rise had amounted to 10 per cent. During 1935 the price-level remained remarkably constant, the index for December being 81.

It had been expected by the promoters of the revaluation policy that the lowering of the value of the dollar in terms of gold would result in a fall of the dollar in relation to commodities, that is to say in a rising price-level. Obviously, however, such a result could only be attained if efficient use were made of the means of payment at disposal. The confidence required for this purpose could not, however, be established so long as the whole economy of the country remained in an experimental stage.

A reduction of the gold par of the dollar may not only lower the value of the dollar in terms of commodities but also raise that of gold. In this case the first effect will be smaller than anticipated. As a matter of fact, President Roosevelt's devaluation did to some extent raise the American price-level but had also the effect of enhancing the value of gold. The London price of gold rose from 130·12 in January 1934 (average of the month) to 136·98 in February the same year, and to 141·8 in January 1935. As the index of general wholesale prices (Board of Trade) remained practically constant during the period, this rise in the price of gold actually denotes an increase of about 9 per cent. in the value of gold in terms of commodities.

The effect upon the countries still adhering to the gold standard was most injurious. They had to go through a further process of deflation, harmful for their economic life in general, but particularly trying for their public finances. France succeeded after the most strenuous efforts in bringing down her price-level from 380 in January 1934 to 342 in January of the following year, that is to say by 10 per cent. Thus the gold parity was preserved, but only at serious sacrifice. Most of the gold countries, however, did not succeed in carrying through such a deflation and, in consequence, had to meet other difficulties, the grave character of which will be clear from the following (§ 26).

Whatever the President may have accomplished by his legislation of January 1934, he certainly did not further his aim of contributing to a solution of the world's monetary problem, and still less to the restoration of an international gold standard. Just as in the case of silver, the President, by arbitrarily raising the price of gold, caused the gold countries unnecessary trouble and even drove them from the gold standard. At the same time his choice of a new gold parity and the motives proclaimed for this choice, together with the prospect of new alterations and of a 'rehabilitation of silver', proved that he did not recognize gold as a standard. Moreover, the President's policy had the effect of making the international distribution of gold still more uneven than it had been before.

Our conclusion must be that by his measures of January 1934 the President neither strengthened the gold standard as such nor furthered its international application. This is, of course, no criticism of his policy; it is a simple statement of fact.

§ 26. *The Gold Bloc*

As we have seen (§ 22) the members of the gold bloc had promised one another assistance in the protection of the gold standard. They had also come to 'complete agreement' as to the means to be used for this purpose. Several meetings of the gold bloc were held to give effect to this decision. The practical programme was, however, limited to two points: (1) furthering trade between the gold countries by abolishing the system of quotas and lowering tariff walls; (2) promoting tourist traffic and improving means of transport. These were sound aims, no doubt, but a little outside the range of the *monetary* problem, for dealing with which the gold bloc had been created. We recognize here the old horror of a purely monetary issue which for so many years had obstructed all honest reconstruction work. The actual situation was this: All gold currencies were overvalued, but in very different degrees. A monetary and economic equilibrium was impossible until this overvaluation had been removed. As long as this monetary task was evaded, any approach to an economic unity between the gold countries was impossible. Moreover, most-favoured-nation clauses stood in the way of any preferential system benefiting the members of the gold bloc. A further important obstacle was the impossibility of conciliating the members' divergent agricultural interests.

When the question arose of giving actual help to members in distress nothing substantial came of the solemn promises of co-operation. Czechoslovakia was forced to devalue her currency in February 1934 and even afterwards had difficulties in maintaining her new gold parity. It is true that, formally, she was not a member of the gold bloc, but her example was ominous.

Belgium had suffered greatly from the process of deflation which the maintenance of the gold standard had forced upon her. She was more dependent than the other members on her export trade; and the paralysis of her exports caused great unemployment. Finally the burden became intolerable, and when even the banking system of the country became endangered, the deflation policy had to be abandoned. In order to cheapen credit and revive business activity several measures were taken, including a scheme of public works. The natural effect was, however, a growing distrust of the currency, and at the beginning of 1935 the monetary situation became more and more serious. The Belgian Prime Minister, M. Teunis, did all in his power to protect the gold par. He even went so far as to institute a system of control for bullion and exchange operations. Things came to a crisis in March 1935, and M. Teunis, together with his most important Ministers, went to Paris to ask for help. When he returned without having secured adequate assistance he was forced to resign, and a new Government was formed under M. van Zeeland, who on 29 March in the Chamber of Deputies announced that the belga was to be devalued by an amount not greater than 30 per cent. and not less than 25 per cent. By a decree published on 31 March the depreciation of the belga was fixed at 28 per cent. Thus Belgium had made a substantial devaluation of her currency, probably large enough to put herself on an equilibrium basis on the world market. This need for a balanced exchange value of the currency proved to be decisive. The country was not forced off the gold standard for lack of gold. Up to the last moment the Central Bank had a gold reserve amounting to 2,259 million belgas against a note circulation of 3,770 millions—which, according to traditional views, should have been amply sufficient to guarantee the maintenance of the gold standard. But this reserve was not used—a further proof—if indeed any more is needed—of the futility of the orthodox doctrine that gold reserves of central banks constitute a guarantee for the redemption of notes and for the payment of demand deposits.

The new gold parity is not very reliable. A further rise in the value of gold would force Belgium to choose between further deflation and repeated devaluation. The latter alternative would sooner or later be preferred. The country might also be tempted to use the abundant gold reserve obtained by the devaluation for creating more money to spend on the perpetual campaign against unemployment, with the consequence of further inflation. It would doubtless have been very much better if Belgium had joined the sterling bloc and fixed a sterling parity as near as possible to the equilibrium level. Such a course would have excluded any reproaches of competition in undervaluation and would have secured for Belgium a quiet place within the world's most important group of trading countries. Why this step was not taken it is difficult to see. No doubt England could have made greater efforts to attract a new member and thus have strengthened the sterling bloc. But the monetary authorities in London hardly displayed sufficient interest in such a solution; British tariff policy was certainly not very encouraging for Belgium in her distress.

Italy had fought a long and hard battle in defence of her gold standard. She had carried through a process of deflation which had brought down her price-level from an average of 654 for 1926 to a minimum of 273 for July 1934. The dictatorship under which Italy is governed exerted all its powers to make the deflation effective and comprehensive. Yet, the battle had to be given up. After the middle of 1934 the price-level began to rise, and an ever stricter control of the exchange value of the lira was introduced. In connexion with the Abyssinian War, private Italian assets in foreign countries were confiscated, and the gold reserve of the Bank of Italy began to be used for the import of war materials. Italy is now actually off the gold standard, although she seeks to conceal this fact by officially pegging the lira. Nobody can tell what the value of the lira will be at the end of the Abyssinian adventure.

After these events only four countries, Poland, Switzerland, Holland, and France, actually stand as defendants of an international gold-standard system.

Poland deflated her currency most energetically and thus succeeded in maintaining its gold par, but only at the cost of reducing her industrial production to the lowest relative level of any country for which an index of production is published.[1]

Switzerland gave up further deflation as early as the beginning of 1933. In spite of a tremendous overvaluation of her currency Switzerland, aided by her large foreign assets, has been able to maintain the gold standard, but only at a ruinous cost. Exports were seriously curtailed. In particular the watch industry suffered an enormous shrinkage, the value of its exports being reduced from 307 million Swiss francs in 1929 to 86 millions in 1932. The country also lost a great part of its income from foreign tourists. There was much agitation against the maintenance of the gold standard and against the trying process of adaptation that it continually demanded, and the opposition forced a referendum on that question (2 June 1935). The opposition was defeated, but not by a large majority. The programme of the opposition was not confined to the monetary question alone but included economic reforms of an extremist character. The result of the vote is there-

[1] *World Economic Survey*, League of Nations, Geneva, 1935, p. 115.

fore hardly a reliable expression of Swiss opinion with regard to monetary policy. The difference between the internal and external value of the Swiss franc is becoming more and more conspicuous.

The necessity for continued deflation caused Holland particular difficulties, inasmuch as the Netherlands East Indian trade suffered heavy losses. Holland has, however, defended her gold standard under the leadership of unusually strong men, such as the Prime Minister, Mr. Collijn, and the Governor of the Central Bank, Mr. Trip. Deflation has been carried much farther than in Switzerland, but the Netherlands currency remains considerably overvalued and the whole economic situation of the country is unstable.

France has pursued her policy of deflation with sacrifices worth a better goal; but this policy has never been quite consistent. Great efforts have been made to maintain high prices for agricultural products, and vast plans for public works have been started. Whereas average wholesale prices have been radically cut down, the cost of living has remained at a high level and money wages still higher. *The World Economic Survey* gives the index numbers (base: 1929 = 100): for wholesale prices as 65 for January 1934 and 53 for March 1935; for cost of living, 95, 94, and 93 as averages for the years 1932, 1933, and 1934. With the same base year the index for hourly money wages stands at 104 throughout the years 1932–4. Thus the whole economy of the country has been brought into a glaring disequilibrium. In addition it has proved almost impossible to balance the budget. Every endeavour to support the gold standard by further deflation has been followed by a loss of public income, a curtailment of production and trade, and growing expenditure on unemployment. The wisdom of such a policy has sometimes been questioned, and from the beginning of 1935 an opposite course was tried, particularly in the form of credit expansion and reduction of interest rates. This experiment would undoubtedly have forced the country to devaluate, but it soon had to be given up as it could not obtain the necessary support from the Bank of France. In May, chiefly in consequence of budgetary difficulties, the franc was again in danger, and the Bank of France repeatedly had to raise its discount rate (finally up to 6 per cent.) and to restrict credit. In addition, it had to part with gold to an amount of some 9,000 million francs in order to protect the gold parity. The Government had to resign and a period of alarming political unrest followed. At last M. Laval, as Prime Minister, resumed a severe policy of deflation and made strenuous efforts to cut down State expenditure and balance the budget. For this purpose he secured for himself extraordinary dictatorial powers during the parliamentary recess, but had later on, to face strong opposition in Parliament, which seriously endangered his budget. Gold again began to pour out and the Bank once more had to raise its discount rate to extraordinary levels. At the same time, however, M. Laval, by one of his decrees, increased the expenditure allocated to the public works schemes from Frs. 2,984 millions to 4,241 millions, and in this way accelerated the public works programme—obviously a measure contrary to the policy of deflation. The official index of wholesale prices reached a minimum of 327 for July 1935 (1913 = 100), but after that time rose again and for December attained the level of 350. Thus the deflationary programme cannot be carried out systematically, but continually exposes France to severe economic and political disturbances. Quieter conditions are unthinkable until the monetary problem has found a real solution.

In France, however, no monetary stabilization is possible so long as the country remains unable to balance its budget reliably. True, the budget for 1936, as approved by Parliament at the end of the old year, was formally balanced, but very considerable deficits are expected to arise, and in addition there is a huge extraordinary budget to be covered by borrowing. The Government has taken powers to raise 15,000 million francs during 1936 by the issue of treasury bills. Such finance is bound to lead to an enforced devaluation, which will perhaps have to be repeated once in every decade and which is at any rate quite a different thing from a deliberate and rational devaluation on sound monetary principles.

Since Great Britain abandoned the gold standard French monetary thinking has been entirely dominated by the single idea that sterling was wilfully depreciated and that England and the sterling bloc at large forced upon France the disagreeable necessity of a continued deflation. French policy has persistently pursued the aim of inducing the paper-standard countries to 'stabilize', which in French means to fix a gold parity. At first France tried discriminating tariffs and later on a system of quotas as a weapon against the paper countries. The result was meagre, and at the London Conference France concentrated her attention upon attaining some international agreement for a restoration of the gold standard. However, the analysis of the problem was fallacious, and the medicine recommended would not have cured the ills from which the world was suffering.

The only reasonable measure of the value of a currency is its purchasing-power against commodities. On this basis England has not depreciated her currency, the annual average price index of the Board of Trade shows an almost complete stability since 1931. What has happened is that gold has risen in value in terms of commodities. This rise can approximately be measured by the rise of the price of gold in London from the old par of about 85 shillings to an average of 142·11 shillings for 1935, that is to say by about two-thirds. This extraordinary enhancement of the value of gold has been the principal factor in the monetary troubles of the countries which have retained their gold parity. The cause of the rise in the value of gold is obviously an enormous increase in the demand for the metal. We shall revert to a discussion of this demand (§ 28). It suffices to state here that the gold countries are themselves chiefly responsible for the destructive competition for gold. How little this truth is understood was strikingly demonstrated when France in 1935 tried to strengthen her gold standard by the curious measure of issuing new gold coins on a large scale! This gold was doomed to disappear in the traditional French stockings and the scarcity of gold could only be increased. The resultant tendency to enhance the value of gold was simply overlooked.

The old monetary orthodoxy has proved entirely misleading. It was generally taught that the gold standard had to be guaranteed by gold reserves and that the larger the gold reserves the better the security. Experience has proved that this is fallacious. Endeavours to strengthen the gold standard by accumulating enormous stocks of gold may lead to a rise in the value of gold that forces gold-standard countries to an intolerable deflation, endangers their budgetary equilibrium and their entire economic life, and perhaps ends with the abandonment of the gold standard. An international gold-standard system is unacceptable so long as it is exposed to such disturbances. If, in the present crisis, the leading gold countries had parted with their unnecessary gold stocks they would in all probability have been able to raise the general price-level in terms of gold to such an extent as to bring the crisis to an end. If they think such an experiment too risky they have no other escape from the crisis than to revalue their currencies in proportion to the rise in the value of gold—or to abandon gold as a standard and join the sterling bloc.

The gold countries suffer from an overvaluation of their currencies. To cure this evil by a deflation that raises the internal value of the currency is not a very promising policy if the factors behind the overvaluation remain in force. An increased internal value is itself a factor tending to raise the international valuation of the currency. It is indeed a very remarkable fact that after a deflation pursued for years the overvaluation of the gold currencies continues, although in the case of France it has been reduced.[1]

[1] I have discussed this subject more fully in the *Skand. Quarterly* of January and October 1935.

From whatever side we view the monetary problem of the gold-standard countries we find that they are themselves responsible for its solution. They would do better to recognize this responsibility than to waste time on blaming the sterling countries for the alleged instability of their paper standards.

When the gold bloc asks the members of the sterling bloc to 'stabilize', it is recommending, as has been said above, a false cure. If sterling countries were to fix new gold parities in accordance with the ruling rates of exchange the fundamental disequilibrium in the present exchange system would be preserved. No other level of exchanges that the sterling bloc could choose would establish a satisfactory equilibrium so long as the mutual exchanges between the gold countries themselves remain far from a true balance. Nor can any exchange equilibrium possess reliable stability if it is based on a metal so variable in value as gold has proved to be. Thus the importunate request for 'stabilization' is hardly more than an empty phrase.

Nevertheless, France continues to urge the paper countries to 'stabilize'. During 1935 M. Bonnet, as Minister of Commerce, has continued to advance this request and to back it up with a more and more threatening trade policy. France, he has declared, is now quite willing to enter upon a more liberal trade policy. But this offer is made conditional upon the willingness of other countries to guarantee the stability of their currencies at definite gold parities. From now on France will demand in every economic agreement the insertion of this currency stability clause.

This programme, which, from the French point of view, seems quite natural, is in reality open to grave objections. No clear-sighted Government can promise to maintain its currency at an invariable parity with gold if the value of gold continues to be subject to violent and incalculable variations. A certain stability of the purchasing-power of the currency in terms of commodities must be the focal point of any rational monetary programme. Secondly, when France insists upon stable relations between foreign currencies and the franc as a condition for liberal trade agreements, other countries must ask themselves whether they on their side can rely on the stability of the franc in terms of gold. The question has only to be put to make us realize that this is a major element of insecurity in trade relations with France. As long as the fate of the French currency is dependent upon a vote of confidence in a French Government, it is impossible to regard the franc as a trustworthy basis for an international currency system.

Obviously, the gold bloc can have no greater stability than the French franc. No country can assume the position of a leader of an international monetary system unless it is capable of so safely balancing its budget that its currency will not be exposed to dangers arising out of financial difficulties. In this respect the gold bloc is an extremely weak construction.

§ 27. *The Sterling Bloc*

The sterling bloc must be said to have been a great success in so far as it has proved the possibility of maintaining stability in a paper-standard system. This possibility had been very generally denied, and even to-day is often denied in spite of all the remarkable experience that has accumulated. Since the formation of the sterling bloc the British wholesale price-level has been kept almost invariable. The rates of exchange between the several members of the sterling bloc have likewise been maintained at a satisfactory stability.

British economic life has greatly benefited from this stability. Considerable recovery has taken place, and industrial relations have been unusually free from labour disputes. These advantages have to a large extent been shared by other members of the sterling bloc, which has also been joined more or less definitely by outside countries such as Argentina, Japan, and China.[1] The essential practical achievement

[1] Since 19 January 1934 Argentina has maintained an official buying rate of 15 paper pesos to the pound, whereas the actual sale rates have fluctuated around 18. The yen, which at the time of the

of the sterling bloc is, however, the rescuing of its members from a continued deflation the devastating effects of which have been so conspicuous in the gold countries.

On the other hand, the programme of the sterling bloc has not been fulfilled in so far as a moderate rise in the general price-level was stated to be the immediate aim of the monetary policy of the bloc. This rise, according to the programme, should proceed as far as was required for re-establishing an equilibrium between costs and prices. At the time of the formation of the bloc the discrepancy to be overcome was certainly no small one. It may have been reduced to some extent during the succeeding years by the continual process of adaptation. But there can hardly be any doubt that a considerable rise in wholesale prices is still needed for restoring a satisfactory equilibrium and that this would have a very beneficial effect.

Why has this point been neglected? The responsible authorities will no doubt answer that they have done everything in their power by their cheap money policy, and that they cannot control the price-level. It is, however, impossible to suppress the doubt whether more could not have been accomplished if the price-raising policy had received the unreserved support of the Bank of England. This has not been

London Conference stood at about 15*d.*, has, since October 1934, been kept practically stable at a rate of 14*d.* As to China, see § 24.

the case and could hardly be expected to be so. The Bank has never endorsed the sterling bloc programme and has shown much more interest in maintaining stable relations to the gold currencies with a view to a prompt restoration of the gold standard. The emphatic pronunciations of the Bank of International Settlements in favour of such a policy seem to leave no doubt as to the views prevailing in the Bank of England.

On this point the *World Economic Survey* (p. 68) makes the following remarkable observation:

> 'Nor have monetary and economic policies', in the sterling countries, 'been always consistently directed towards an effort to raise the average level of prices. Most of them have combined external depreciation with an effort to make domestic credit abundant and cheap; but many elements of both credit and general economic policy have been directly or indirectly of a deflationary character. Thus the building-up of larger gold reserves, the reduction of the fiduciary issue, and the strict budgetary policies pursued in the United Kingdom have tended to keep domestic prices from rising.'

There are several other signs of such a tendency. For years expenditure on public works above the minimum of necessary replacement was eschewed, and issues of new loans on the London market were severely restricted. It is a gross misunderstanding to regard this weakness of the monetary policy as being counterbalanced by the various measures undertaken in England to restrict the supply of commodities. As has been pointed out in § 13, the aim of monetary policy should be to provide the mechanism for handling a *growing* supply of commodities at a stable price-level, and, in the present case, even at a somewhat improved price-level.

The foremost effect—though one that is often overlooked—of stopping the process of deflation is a revival of the producer's confidence. A guarantee that prices will not further be depressed by monetary policy will go a long way to induce him to new enterprise. This effect will naturally be most conspicuous in the building trade and other industries representing long-term investment. When at the same time monetary policy is reversed from high to low interest rates, such production will receive a powerful stimulus. These effects will of course be still more strengthened if an actual rise of prices takes place. But even without such a rise, the factors mentioned must be expected to bring about a change from depression to recovery.

The truth of this reasoning has been amply demonstrated by the experience of the sterling bloc compared with that of the gold bloc. Up to the time of the London Conference there had been in both groups some revival of industrial activity. Since the second quarter of 1933 the gold countries experienced a rapid fall in their industrial activity and the sterling bloc an equally rapid rise. The disparity in the development is indeed striking, the index of industrial activity for the second quarter (average 1929 = 100) having fallen in France from 85·8 in 1933 to 66·5 in 1935, but having risen in the United Kingdom from 91·7 to 103·9 and in Sweden from 82·1 to 108·2. The impression of the advantage of the sterling system is overwhelming.

Within the sterling bloc, exchange stability, relative freedom of trade, and some renewal of international lending also contributed to recovery.

Governments generally flatter themselves that their intervention in economic life in the form of public works, subsidies, and all sorts of control has been very effective and is entitled to the chief credit for any improvement achieved. These claims are dubious, and, as they are raised by the most divergent political systems, they can hardly be taken to support any one of them in particular. Surveying the world as a whole, we must come to the conclusion that during the present depression the net result of all government interference in the economic sphere is negative. This observation may serve further to emphasize the fundamentally important part that sound monetary policy has played in such recovery as has actually taken place.

The fact that such a paper-standard system as the sterling bloc has actually come into being, confutes the old dogmatic view that stability in an international monetary system is possible only on a gold basis.[1] Those who still adhere to such views have therefore been at pains to show that the sterling bloc also has its weak sides. It has been pointed out that countries greatly dependent on the export of certain special commodities might easily be driven off their present pound parities were the conditions of this export to be rendered more unfavourable. It is, in fact, not difficult to imagine economic conditions that would compel Denmark or Australia or New Zealand, for instance, to reduce the pound parities of their currencies. But this is a risk that is inherent in any international monetary system and which a gold standard could not prevent—as has been well illustrated by the devaluation in Czechoslovakia and in Belgium. The existence of this risk is indeed a wholesome reminder that a certain stability in the conditions for international commerce and distribution of production is a *sine qua non* for stability in the monetary system.

The success of the sterling bloc is so evident that a further consolidation and extension of this monetary system, combined with the perfecting of its monetary policy, is generally regarded as all that its members can desire, at least for the present. True, a return to an international gold standard is officially

[1] See my article in the *Skand. Quarterly*, October 1935.

spoken of in general terms as the 'ultimate aim'—always, however, with the reservation that the conditions for a normal working of the gold standard must be fulfilled. This reservation suggests a profound doubt as to whether such a state of things will ever be attained. There is, of course, in England a certain desire to stabilize the Paris rate of exchange. But this desire is more directed towards smoothing out temporary fluctuations than towards regulating the exchange at variance with fundamental tendencies. England is certainly not willing to sacrifice her newly won monetary independence and expose sterling to the uncertainties of the international gold market or to the incalculable use of foreign gold reserves in the service of political power. In fact, we have all reason to look upon England's abandonment of the gold standard as having developed into something much more definite than the original emergency measure. Time is bound to work for the sterling standard, if this standard is only administered with a clear conception of the kind of monetary policy that *economic* welfare demands.

In his principal address to the London Conference the Chancellor of the Exchequer emphasized that such a policy ought to be 'clearly announced and vigorously pursued'. It would be too much to say that the expectations awakened by these words have been fully realized. On this point Sir Basil Blackett, in his contribution to the Sterling Bloc Supplement of the *Daily Telegraph*, 8 July 1935, made the following observation:

'Since the departure from the gold standard the Government has proceeded, quite rightly, to forget the Gold Standard in practice, and to give the nation the blessings of a managed currency, though denying both its desire and its ability to undertake the task of management.'

The real strength of the sterling system can certainly be manifested more clearly than has been done hitherto.

IX

THE ILLUSION OF A RETURN TO GOLD

§ 28. *The Supposed Need for Gold Reserves*

OUR investigation has shown how thoroughly the whole gold-standard system has been destroyed and how unpromising are the prospects of any future revival of that system. Gold has failed, both as a means of payment and as a standard of value. The situation at the end of 1935 puts this fact in the most merciless light and deserves to be surveyed with a view to ascertaining what is the actual place of gold in the monetary system of to-day. Such a survey will confirm our previous conclusions and give an opportunity to summarize them. It is convenient to examine the functioning of gold first as a reserve and then as a standard.

Do our gold reserves really serve any sensible purpose? An outsider who came from another planet and observed the present behaviour of humanity in regard to gold would hardly come to the conclusion that the huge gold stocks which we have accumulated with so much toil, sacrifice, and fighting were of much use to us. However, in the traditional gold-standard doctrine that still dominates current ideas of money, gold fulfils an essential function as a means of payment or as a basis for other means of payment.

We have, then, firstly to state the fact that for *internal* payments gold has practically ceased to be used in physical form and is of no real importance as a reserve. Indeed, so far as the home market is concerned, the idea that gold is needed as a reserve against liabilities of central banks should have lost ground fairly completely in a society that does not recognize any private ownership of monetary gold, or in which central banks are not obliged to supply gold for internal use, or, at any rate, cannot be trusted to do so unconditionally. Is it not time, in face of these facts, to weed text-books of the traditional representation of gold reserve as a 'cover' for the note circulation or as 'something tangible behind it'? In view of the actual situation the time must also be ripe for scrapping the whole mass of old-fashioned legislation fixing minimum reserves in some arbitrary arithmetical relation to the note circulation, or, more generally, to central bank liabilities. There is no reason why monetary legislation should always be determined by the ideas and superstitions of a past century.

Present-day gold-standard theory seeks to escape this criticism by placing the use of gold reserves for *international* settlements in the foreground, and teaches that the only function of a gold reserve is to iron out discrepancies in the current balance of payments of the country. This widely accepted view seems to have very little foundation in investigations of actual facts. In the case of Sweden I have made such an investigation, which refutes the belief that gold is needed for paying temporary deficits in the current international balance.[1] The gold movements that have occurred have simply been caused by the demand for gold reserves, at home or abroad, and thus far are merely a consequence of these demands. Probably the same holds good, at least approximately, for the world at large. Surely, under normal conditions, a balancing of current payments could in most cases easily be arranged by means of such international credits as form part of everyday transactions.

To keep a gold reserve for ironing out discrepancies in the international balance of payments would presumably be a need mainly for debtor countries. Such countries often borrow gold directly for the purpose; in any case their foreign debt is swelled by their acquirement of gold. To borrow gold funds for meeting possible deficits in future balances of payments can hardly be regarded as a policy warranted to inspire confidence. Whatever may be said of Dr. Schacht's monetary policy and his way of managing the German currency under the Nazi régime he must at any rate be credited with the great merit of having unmasked, once for all, the humbug of 'strengthening' a currency by means of borrowed gold reserves.

But there remain other reasons for keeping gold in

[1] *Skand. Quarterly*, October 1934.

reserve for international payments. Recent gold movements, which in their gigantic dimensions have been an outstanding element of disturbance, are essentially *capital* movements without any connexion with the current balance of trade. Gold has served as a means for a flight of capital from dubious currencies to better trusted ones, or for a transfer of hoards from one country to another, according to varying views of the security offered for such holdings of gold. To a great extent international gold movements result from that excessive and unsound search for liquidity which, as we have seen in § 10, is a consequence of a monetary system in which the ultimate means of payment is a concrete material like gold. Gold is also used for an export of capital seeking profitable investment in other countries. It may be doubted whether it is in the public interest by such an artificial means as the keeping of large gold reserves in the central bank, to facilitate international capital transfers, which ought to be free but self-supporting, i.e. ought to be paid for by a surplus in the balance of payments.

Further, there is always the possibility of consuming gold reserves for emergency needs. Instances are the exhaustion of the Austrian gold reserve during the War and of the German during Germany's post-War food scarcity. In 1935 a considerable part of the Italian gold reserve had been consumed for buying war materials from abroad. Finally, governments find gold reserves useful as a means for exercising political pressure or for buying military assistance.

Whatever may be said in favour of maintaining gold reserves for needs such as those above mentioned, it can hardly be contended that such holding of gold has any necessary connexion with an international system of money built up with the aim of serving normal requirements for means of payment. If we once admit that other requirements than purely monetary ones constitute a ground for holding gold reserves in central banks, there are no limits to the demand for gold; and no reserves, whatever their size, can truly be described as adequate.

When gold reserves are proclaimed to be necessary for balancing current international trade, it seems to be a logical consequence that their size should be determined in some relation to the volume of imports. In such a case a reserve corresponding to the value of imports for some few months should be amply sufficient.

Actual gold reserves show no sign of being regulated in accordance with such a principle. The Economic Committee of the League of Nations presented in September 1935, at the meeting of the Assembly, some 'Remarks on the Present Phase of International Economic Relations' (Geneva, 1935). In this paper certain figures are given regarding gold reserves and the need for them. On 31 July 1934 the world's total gold reserves amounted to 67,250 whilst the aggregate of foreign trade in 1934 was 121,144 (in millions of Swiss francs). Total imports should amount to approximately half the last figure and would therefore be less than the total gold reserve. *In other words, the world actually holds gold reserves to an amount more than sufficient to pay a whole year's imports without any use of the corresponding exports!* If anything can be called madness it is this. If there is no other motive for keeping gold reserves than the need for balancing international trade, the aggregate reserve of the world could easily be reduced to a small fraction of what it is.

Curiously enough, the most striking examples of excessive gold reserves are offered by two great creditor countries, France and the United States. According to the source quoted, France had a foreign trade (in Swiss francs) of 8,306 and kept a gold reserve of 16,675; America's foreign trade had a value of 11,547 and against this was kept a gold reserve amounting to 25,216, which was about five times the year's import. The table gives for 'other countries', not specifically mentioned, aggregate trade as 68,092 and gold reserves as 8,911, which seems to be a much more reasonable proportion. According to this proportion the United States could be satisfied with a gold reserve of 1,450, which, in view of the customary surplus of American exports, would be amply sufficient. Comparing this figure with the actual gold reserve of 25,216 we must draw the conclusion that the need for balancing international trade has nothing to do with American demands for gold reserves.

Nor do the figures endorse the traditional view that large gold reserves increase the security of central banks. At the end of 1929 the aggregate value of the world's note circulation (excluding Russia) was 116,350 and that of gold reserves 55,869 million Swiss francs. At the end of 1934 these figures were 98,470 and 67,250. This fact seems to refute very definitely indeed the orthodox teaching that gold reserves give *robur et securitas*[1] to the currency. Nobody would contend that the currencies of the world were in a safer condition in 1934 than in 1929; and yet the percentage of gold 'cover' had increased from 48 to 70. The truth is that the struggle for strengthening currencies by increasing gold reserves has ended by wrecking the whole gold-standard system and threatening to ruin the countries with the highest gold reserves.

§ 29. *Gold Reserves as a Regulator of Credit*

According to the traditional gold-standard doctrine the supply of bank-notes, or more generally of means

[1] The device of Sweden's Riksbank since 1668.

of payment, ought to be continually regulated by every country so as to correspond to its gold reserve. Such regulation was regarded as the fundamental condition for an adequate distribution of the world's gold as well as for the necessary equalization of price-levels. This rule was deliberately thrust aside by the post-War monetary policy of the United States. The huge additions to American gold reserves were looked upon as temporary deposits which would be withdrawn as soon as normal order had been restored to the world economy. Thus the internal supply of means of payment was regulated with a view to the needs of the American economy, and excess gold reserves were not allowed to effect a corresponding rise of the general price-level. A similar policy was applied later on in other gold countries. This autonomous regulation of the supply of means of payment was in itself quite sound. But it was contrary to the fundamental principle of the international gold-standard system and exposed it to grave danger. The aggregate effect of the accumulations of idle gold reserves in some few countries was that a large part of the world's stock of gold was immobilized and that the scarcity of gold was very much intensified, with a subsequent pressure towards deflation. For this reason, and in order to restore the functioning of the gold standard in conformity with classical rules, the Gold Delegation proposed that 'gold movements should normally be allowed to make their effects felt' and 'that credit should be extended or contracted and money rates modified with a view to righting the balance'.[1] This recommendation has been endorsed by later monetary programmes. A 'statement of principles concerning the operation of an international monetary standard based on gold and the endeavour to contribute to the maintenance of a more constant level of business activity . . . was agreed by central bank representatives, submitted to the London Conference of 1933, and there unanimously adopted' (subject to American reservations).[2]

The second point of this statement reads:

> 'Gold movements so far as they seem to be of a more permanent character should normally not be prevented from making their influence felt both in the country losing gold and in the country receiving gold.'

This, then, must be regarded as the accepted policy of the advocates of a restoration of the gold standard. In the present stage of maldistribution of the world's stock of gold, combined with the extraordinary mobility of gold reserves and the extensive use of them for capital transfers, nothing could have more dangerous and destructive effects on the world economy.

[1] *Second Interim Report of the Gold Delegation*, Geneva, 1931, pp. 17–18.

[2] Bank for International Settlements, *Fifth Annual Report*, Basle, 1935, p. 47.

In recent years fluctuations in gold reserves have been on an enormous scale. In particular the gold movements in 1935 stand out as noteworthy. In the first half of that year the gold reserve of the United States increased by 878 million dollars. In the same period European gold-standard countries lost gold reserves to a relatively much greater extent. In the case of France the loss was 737 million dollars, in that of the Netherlands 146, in that of Switzerland 233. The last figure means a loss of more than a third of the country's gold stock. The fluctuations in the second half of the year were equally disturbing. If the internal supply of means of payment were to be determined by gold reserves exposed to such violent fluctuations, one can only shudder at the thought of the resulting economic disturbances.

Since at the end of January 1934 a new lower gold par was fixed for the dollar, gold has poured into the United States in successive waves, resulting in the increase in the country's monetary gold stock as stated in § 25. Thus the so-called gold 'basis' for the liabilities of the Federal Reserve System was greatly strengthened. In addition, the silver purchases increased the reserve by a very substantial sum. Member bank reserves have increased in a similar proportion and the 'excess reserves' have come up to some 3,000 million dollars. As each dollar of these reserves may serve as a basis for deposits of about

12 dollars, we see that member banks have an almost fantastic margin for widening their credit supply.

Thus a rise in prices is to be expected. In fact, this has been the aim of President Roosevelt's monetary policy, and to a certain extent this aim has already been realized with favourable effects on the nation's economy. One can only wish that this movement could be continued a good deal farther; indeed, this seems to be the policy of the American authorities. In this case, however, there is the danger that what has been a sound recovery may turn into an unbalanced boom. If under such circumstances member banks should grant new credits to the extent allowed by their reserves the consequence would be an enormous inflation. This danger is being eagerly discussed in the United States. The country has a hard-earned experience of the devastation that may follow upon such a development, and it is generally desired that a repetition should be prevented.

What powers does the Federal Reserve System possess for controlling developments? The discount rate is hardly effective when member banks have such huge excess reserves and have practically no need for borrowing. It is true that recent legislation has given the system power to raise the percentage of reserve requirements and thus to reduce excess reserves. Moreover, the system may sell Government securities, of which it had accumulated the extraordinary amount of 2,430 million dollars by the end of November 1935. But it is somewhat doubtful whether use will be made of these powers.

To interrupt a favourable economic development is never popular. Besides, it is difficult to tell when the right moment has come for pulling in. Moreover, the metallic reserve is, according to orthodox doctrine, amply sufficient for a much-extended volume of credit. It will be seen here how fallacious and indeed dangerous is the view that the size of the reserve shall determine the volume of credit, or that the so-called 'percentage cover' should in any way be used as a directive for monetary policy. The great question is whether the American authorities will be able entirely to emancipate themselves from this tradition. They must do so if they are ever to create that dollar which the President dreamt of when he proclaimed a purchasing-power invariable through generations as the criterion of a good dollar. Restrictive measures will, of course, always come in conflict with the Government's financial interests. A selling out of Government securities combined with a higher discount rate would force down quotations and thus hamper the issue of new loans. The present American situation is particularly sensitive in this respect as member banks are heavily engaged in Government stocks. On 1 November 1935 total Government securities of the member banks amounted to 11,844 million dollars. The impossibility of selling such a gigantic stock should be obvious.

The great amount of unemployment, the political situation in general, and in particular the 'veterans'' insistence upon bonus payments, will lead to an increasing demand for means of payment; and this demand will be strengthened by the presence of abundant reserves. These reserves will therefore have a strong influence in tempting the country along the road of a dangerous inflation.

If, on the other hand, European gold-standard countries try to adjust the volume of credit to their sinking gold reserves, they will be driven to further deflation with pernicious effects on their economic life.

Thus the situation at the end of 1935 offers a singularly clear demonstration of the practical necessity for making monetary policy entirely independent of gold reserves. The recommendations of the orthodox gold-standard theory could not be carried out without disastrous results. This patent fact should give the advocates of a restoration of the gold standard a hard nut to crack.

Of course, it may always be said that the principle of adjusting supply of credits to gold reserves can only be applied gradually, and that reasonable time must be allowed for the necessary redistribution of the world's gold stock. The orthodox gold-standard theory is bound to assume an initial situation in which gold reserves are reasonably well balanced. If, then, the rule of adjusting credits to gold reserves is applied, the equilibrium, according to the theory, will be automatically maintained. But can anybody conversant with the present economic conditions of the world, and with the state of mind of monetary authorities and leading politicians, see the slightest hope for such a redistribution of gold reserves as the theory requires? If we keep to actual facts we must recognize that the desire to accumulate the largest possible gold reserves is still as general and as intense as ever. In Japan the annual gold production is estimated at about 90 million yen and an increase is anticipated. The hope is expressed that all this gold will be accumulated in the Bank of Japan and that thus a broad basis will be established for an abundant supply of money. At the same time it is expected that Japanese exports will rise in thirty years to about four times the present amount, and that an annual export balance of more than 4,000 million yen will thereby be attained. It is added that 'such an increase in export and import activity is pre-requisite to the Japan of the future'.[1] Presumably, the huge export surplus would largely be used for an import of gold, thus bringing the reserve up to an immense figure.

[1] *The Oriental Economist*, Tokyo, January 1936.

The fact that such aspirations are entertained should make everybody realize how dangerous is the principle that the supply of means of payments should be adjusted to the gold reserve; also, how entirely the national eagerness for an accumulation of gold is opposed to the idea of an equitable redistribution of the world's gold reserves; and finally, how the most unsound protectionist tendencies are strengthened throughout the world by the insatiable craving for gold that seems to be inseparable from the international gold-standard system.

In formulating his new gold policy President Roosevelt proclaimed, 'This is no time to dissipate gold reserves.' Indeed, if there ever has been a time for 'dissipating gold reserves' it was on that occasion. If those in power refused to do anything for a reasonable redistribution of gold at a moment when the international situation indicated such action as being singularly well grounded, and indeed urgent, there is surely no hope for a better opportunity, nor for a restoration of an international gold-standard system.

In short, an international gold standard requires that the principle of adjusting credit to gold reserves should be put into effect. On the other hand, under present conditions the application of this principle is practically impossible in view of the extraordinary maldistribution of gold reserves and of the dominating use of gold for capital transfers. Here is a conflict that at least must be clearly perceived. It is by no means of a merely temporary nature, and there is no way out of it.

Under the stimulus of the higher prices paid for gold in terms of sterling, gold production has greatly increased during the last few years. According to the *World Economic Survey*, 1935 (p. 249), the total gold production was in 1934 approximately 40 per cent. higher than in 1929. The sum of monetary gold reserves for which figures are published grew in the same period by something between 20 and 25 per cent. These reserves would be very much increased by a revaluation in accordance with the actual gold value of the currencies. The *Survey* estimates that after such revaluation the total gold reserve of the world would be at least 75 per cent. higher than it was five years ago. Considering how much the price-level has fallen in the same period this reserve should suffice for supporting any desirable volume of credit. The *Survey* expresses the opinion 'that the danger of a shortage of gold for monetary purposes in the near future has disappeared and that ample reserves are available to support a much larger volume of credit than is at present in use'.

It is also widely believed that a general return to the gold standard would give rise to such confidence in the monetary system that hoarded gold would flow back to the central banks and that in this way the gold reserves would receive another and very important addition. As, however, recent Western hoarding largely corresponds to dispersion of hoards in India and the Far East, account must be taken of the possibility that gold will flow back to Eastern hoards. Moreover, it is by no means certain that the reconstructed gold-standard system would inspire so much confidence that it would be able to attract much gold from private hoards. A reconstructed gold-standard system could doubtless reckon with an abundance of gold reserves—to begin with. But this abundance would probably be followed by a large and progressive increase in the volume of credit and by a subsequent rise of the general price-level. In view of the tremendous amount of unemployment still to be overcome and of the strong pressure towards an increase in Government expenditure in general, it can hardly be doubted that the development would go a long way in that direction. The *Survey* says (p. 276): 'Currency depreciation and devaluation have increased the world's monetary resources so greatly that there must eventually be a considerable rise in prices and, unless effective measures can be devised in the meantime to check undue credit expansion, another unbalanced industrial boom may follow.' When in this way the classical principle of an adjustment of the volume of credit to gold reserves is rejected, another principle for the regulation of credit must be found. But then gold is dethroned from its position as a regulator of the supply of means of payment.

If, on the other hand, prices were allowed to rise in proportion to the growing gold reserves, these reserves would no longer be found to be abundant in relation to the demand. Moreover, gold production would be hampered by rising costs, and the ultimate result would be a new scarcity of gold with subsequent credit restrictions. The world would have had a boom period, only to be thrown again into a deflation crisis. Thus revaluation is no reliable or lasting means for securing sufficient gold reserves.

Clearly, the only way to a permanent stabilization of the world's monetary system is to make the supply of credit entirely independent of the gold reserves of central banks.

§ 30. *Gold as a Standard*

According to the *Encyclopaedia Britannica*, 'Standard' means 'a fixed weight, measure, value or quality established by law or customarily recognized as a unit of comparison by which the correctness of others can be determined'.

Thus if gold is made a standard of value this means that an invariable gold parity is chosen as the criterion of stability of our monetary unit. We may, nevertheless, be aware of the fact that the value of gold in terms of commodities is variable, and even be conscious of the harmful effects of such variations. But in accepting gold as a standard, we deliberately decide to disregard the possibility of changes in the value of gold. If the prospect, now so frequently held out, of a near or 'ultimate' return to the gold standard has any true meaning, it must be that currencies should be recognized as stable in so far as they remain stable in terms of gold.

This conclusion is by no means generally accepted. The programmes for a restoration of the gold standard are often coupled with recommendations for a policy aiming at stabilizing the value of gold itself. Such recommendations can have a logical sense only if some other measure of value is taken as a standard. Moreover, some restoration programmes regard a more or less violent change in the value of gold in relation to commodities as a reason for adjusting existing gold parities. This means, however, that gold is actually dethroned from its position as a standard, and that we have to agree on some other standard of monetary stability.

We see here that the popular and seemingly quite simple recommendations for a return to the gold standard suffer from a fundamental weakness, which cannot be ignored. This reminder is particularly appropriate when pretentious international plans for monetary stabilization have been laid before the public in such number and variety as has been the case in 1935. Most of these plans are superficial and limit themselves to a plea for the restoration of the gold standard without any serious investigation of the meaning of this programme, the conditions for its realization, or the difficulties that must be overcome. Often the danger of great and calamitous changes in the value of gold is disregarded, as if silence on this vital point would avert the hazards. These deficiencies have been conspicuous in the resolutions and recommendations presented during the year by great international conferences and organizations.

In March the Carnegie Endowment for International Peace held an international conference in London with an imposing list of representative members. This conference recommended 'that the leading Governments, especially in the first instance those of France, Great Britain, and the United States, should consult one another without delay for the purpose of coming to a provisional stabilization of exchange on the basis of gold—allowing for the possibility of readjustment in case of need—with a view to the establishment of a stable world gold standard'.

The Bank for International Settlements in their annual report, presented in May, proclaimed as the first aim of central bank co-operation, 'the restoration and the maintenance of a stable international monetary system based on gold'. It was added that 'central banks perceive the defects of the gold standard as disclosed by the past . . .' and 'recognize that an international gold standard is a living, not a static thing, and that the lessons of continuing experience are capable of improving it'. The report also says that it is 'an appropriate goal of central bank policy to attempt to reduce undue fluctuations in the purchasing power of gold, and thus to contribute towards bringing about a greater measure of stability in the value of money'.

The International Chamber of Commerce held a congress in Paris in June and had for this occasion prepared a report recommending the re-establishment of 'a stable international monetary standard', which in the opinion of the Chamber must 'be a freely functioning gold standard'. Although the report treated this subject at some length, it failed to explain in definite terms the real meaning of a restoration of gold as a standard. The report speaks of a general rise in prices as desirable, but expects it to result from economic forces—based on the new confidence which stabilization would inspire—and disregards the change in the value of gold, which is the reverse side of a rise in gold prices. If a general rise in prices is part of our reconstruction programme we cannot truly say that gold is our standard of value; on the contrary, the attainment and stabilization of a certain price-level is set up as our standard for sound monetary policy.

Further, the Chamber's recommendation of the gold standard as a 'stable' standard cannot but appear daring and irresponsible in view of the great changes in the value of gold that have taken place in recent times, and in view of the absolutely incalculable future of that value. A particularly instructive example is afforded by the variations that the Netherlands' currency has undergone since 1926. According to the new weighted price-index of the Central Statistical Bureau, food sank in value from 106·8 as the average of 1926 to 63·2 for July 1935. At the same time raw materials for the food industry sank from 104·9 to 33·1 and all raw materials from 103·0 to 42·0, whilst the general price-index fell only from 105·8 to 60·6. This revolution in prices took place in a country that had remained 'faithful to the gold standard'. Can any one honestly represent such a standard as being 'stable?'

At the Assembly of the League of Nations in September the monetary problem was dealt with in a report by the Second Committee. The Committee states that in their debates 'the general feeling was entirely in favour of the restoration of a stable purchasing power of currency, both internal and external'. To explain the meaning of this statement the

Committee quotes the following words from a report of the Economic Committee:

'All are agreed that the final object must be the re-establishment of a stable international monetary standard—that is, the gold standard, "which remains the best available monetary mechanism".'

How 'stable purchasing power of currency' is to be attained under the rule of the gold standard is a question that is left in impenetrable darkness.

In the United States 'The Economists' National Committee on Monetary Policy' published a collection of statements as to the restoration of the gold standard. In the first of these statements, dated 24 November 1933, it is said: 'While we recognize that the gold standard, as it has heretofore existed, is far from a perfect standard, it is the best standard . . .'; and further: 'An early return to the gold standard and co-operation with other nations for the improvement of that standard are desirable . . .'. If an improvement is thought desirable there must obviously be some independent standard for gauging this improvement. Thus gold is not recognized as the ultimate standard.

We see that the same contradiction constantly recurs in these public proclamations in favour of the gold standard. The real problem to be solved has not been perceived, still less thoroughly examined.

In 1935 private economists contributed some important papers in favour of a restoration of the gold standard. The first of these papers was 'The Road to Recovery' published by Sir Henry Strakosch at the beginning of the year as a supplement to *The Economist*. This remarkable study probably presents the case for a restoration of the gold standard in the best possible form. The most immediate and in fact dominating task is, according to Sir Henry, 'the restoration of a stable equilibrium between the costs of production and the prices of the goods produced and between the burden of debts and incomes'. In the gold countries this can be accomplished only by 'an appropriate reduction of the gold value of their currencies'. (Here it must be observed that another and better way is open to them, namely, to abandon the gold standard and to join the sterling bloc.)

If we assume that every country has established, by an adequate raising of its price-level, a fair internal equilibrium, the way would be open for restoration of exchange stability over a wide area and for the 'resumption of a freer and fuller flow of international trade and lending'. The world would then 'have brought nearer the possibility of re-establishing an International Gold Standard'.

If the reconstruction of the world's monetary system must pass through the first two stages here mentioned—as it is obviously bound to do—we must ask, What is the use of the third stage? The practical problem before us is to secure internal as well as international equilibrium in our monetary system. If the end has been attained by means of rational managing, aided by international co-operation, this method has proved its efficiency, and it should be superfluous afterwards to give the monetary system a new basis by such an artificial measure as connecting it with gold. In fact, it is not only superfluous, it is dangerous, inasmuch as it gives rise to fresh disturbances the serious character of which should be patent enough to every attentive student of post-War monetary history.

Sir Henry Strakosch seems to think that a general devaluation of gold currencies to 60 per cent. of the former gold value is recommendable. Very likely, however, the figure is merely taken for the sake of simplification. In reality, there are substantial *relative* disequilibria between the gold countries, and their needs for devaluation are very different.

A general devaluation down to 60 per cent. would therefore cause new, and at the first moment doubtless serious, disequilibria and, in particular, would require a large amount of inflation in such a country as France, where a severe deflation has already been carried through. Such a reflation would necessitate far-reaching adjustments in the economy of the country, and it would take a considerable time to reach a new equilibrium of sufficient reliability, in regard to internal as well as international relations. A devaluation of the gold currencies is indeed not such a simple task as it is often assumed to be in public discussion.

On the assumption, however, that all countries return to a gold standard with adequate gold parities for their currencies, the revaluation of gold reserves will lead to a superabundant supply of gold. Sir Henry Strakosch calculates that after such revaluation the supply of gold would be sufficient for normal economic progress during the next generation, and herein he sees a guarantee for the maintenance of the new gold-standard system. But, as we have seen in section 29, this guarantee is nothing to rely upon as rising prices would gradually increase the need for means of payment. Indeed, there is a serious danger that the redundancy of gold would cause a violent rise in prices with fresh disturbances of the world economy. Sir Henry Strakosch is, however, of the opinion that this danger can be avoided if the United States and France continue their 'traditional policy of sterilizing a very large part of their superabundant gold reserves'. Thus the stability of the new gold-standard system would essentially depend upon the willingness of two countries to continue an irrational and very costly tradition of gold hoarding. It is impossible to say that this prospect is likely to inspire much confidence in the system, especially as the recommendation of such hoarding stands in contradiction to the orthodox rule according to which full use should be made of gold reserves.

In order to support his programme for a restoration of the gold standard Sir Henry Strakosch emphasizes 'the faith which people the world over have shown in gold as a safe refuge for their cash resources'. It has been shown here that the faith in gold is something quite different from the faith in a gold standard, and that no future gold standard will offer any security for redemption in gold or even for the maintenance of a fixed gold parity. Under such circumstances it is hardly possible to argue that the gold standard has an inherent quality commanding general confidence, or is the only monetary system that possesses this distinction.

In other programmes published by notable economists in 1935 the idea of a provisional stabilization in terms of gold was predominant. In the middle of July, at the invitation of the Antwerp Chamber of Commerce, economists from various countries met to discuss monetary stabilization. There was a minority which gave an orthodox and unqualified support to the gold standard. The majority, which included the three British representatives, Messrs. Keynes, Henderson, and Harrod, and the Swedish Professor Ohlin, found a devaluation of currencies of the gold bloc to be an indispensable precondition for any stabilization. In compensation the other countries should promise not to 'depreciate' their currencies any further. At this point it must be remarked that sterling has not been 'depreciated', nor have the currencies attached to sterling. The fact that gold has appreciated in terms of sterling is nothing for which the sterling countries can be made responsible. The positive programme of the majority is essentially characterized by two proposals. Firstly, when new gold parities have been fixed in better correspondence to economic equilibrium, the system should allow a considerably wider margin for the movements of exchanges than was usual in the pre-War gold-standard system, in which the distance between the gold points was kept at a minimum. Secondly, if experience should prove that a fixed parity did not really correspond, or no longer corresponded, to a true equilibrium, this parity should be given up and replaced by a new one. Similar views were advanced by Sir Arthur Salter in two articles contributed to the *Economist* in August.

There are some serious objections to these programmes.

Provisional stabilization seems to be a rather dubious proposal. Its very essence is a rejection of gold as a standard. Another standard must be set up by which the expediency of an eventual change of the gold parity should be judged. Such a standard is, for example, that of the British monetary programme at the London Conference, viz. after a preliminary rise of the general price-level, a stabilization of that price-level. If this objective cannot be attained on the basis of a given gold parity, the gold parity has to be changed. Another standard may be a general equilibrium of exchange rates. For instance, if a country's rate on London obviously deviates from the purchasing-power parity, or, more generally, from the true equilibrium rate, this is acknowledged as a sufficient reason for altering the gold parity. Thus monetary policy will continually have to fulfil its two main aims, namely, to provide the countries with a money of stable purchasing-power and to adjust rates of exchange to an equilibrium level. The realization of these aims can only be made more difficult by provisionally linking up the currency with gold and thus placing the monetary policy of the country in the position of having to break its connexion with gold as soon as the gold parity chosen is found to be incompatible with the ultimate objectives of the administration of the currency. Such an obligation may unduly postpone action, awaken distrust, and thus cause unnecessary disturbances.

Moreover, the fixation of a provisional gold parity will inevitably call forth a speculation in gold. The prospective adjustment of the gold parity will in practice—to judge from accumulated experience—always be an adjustment downwards. There is thus a balance of probability that the gold parity of the currency will sooner or later be reduced. This probability is bound to lead to a hoarding of gold, which will naturally become more marked in any period of economic or political unrest. The consequence will be a rise in the value of gold, with the result that the maintenance of the gold parity will be subjected to new difficulties and perhaps will have to be given up. Thus a provisional gold standard is like a safety-valve that has been misconstructed and works in the wrong direction.[1]

If anybody imagines the danger of repeated devaluations to be a mere theoretical invention, he ought to remember that France made a very substantial devaluation as late as in 1928 and yet is expected sooner or later to surrender to a new one; that Belgium has already formally devalued twice; and that the heavily devalued Italian currency is at present rapidly losing so much in value that a new and very considerable devaluation is unavoidable if the lira is ever again to be tied to gold.

§ 31. *The Way to Stability*

In the *Lloyds Bank Monthly* (Oct. 1935) Mr. Keynes published an article on 'The Future of the Foreign Exchanges', in which he developed

[1] See my article, 'The Actual Trend of Monetary Development', *Skand. Quarterly*, October 1935.

somewhat more in detail his programme for a provisional gold standard. 'The first condition', he says, 'which must be satisfied before it is worth while to discuss permanent policy, is that the *de facto* rates of exchange, from which we start out, should be in reasonable equilibrium.' In regard to this question it is necessary to observe that the establishment of *internal* price equilibrium, which formed part of the British monetary programme of the London Conference and on which Sir Henry Strakosch rightly lays so much stress, must precede, at least in principle, any stabilization of exchanges. If the general price-level in a particular country is too low, it must be raised so far as may be required to re-establish equilibrium between commodity prices and cost of production. A similar adjustment of internal price-levels—upwards or downwards—must be accomplished in all countries concerned. Equilibrium rates of exchange essentially depend on the general levels of commodity prices in the several countries and cannot be determined until these price-levels have themselves reached a reasonable equilibrium.

Mr. Keynes rejects the purchasing-power parity theory based on wholesale-price index numbers, and gives a long list of other factors to be considered in calculating equilibrium exchange rates. From the outset I have recognized that there are such other factors, and a reference to them does not invalidate my exposition of the purchasing-power parity theory.[1] Nor can the analysis of the problem of international exchanges be greatly furthered by a mere pell-mell enumeration of disconnected factors, including such imponderable things as 'those tariffs, &c., which are a permanent feature of national policies', or 'the probable readiness and ability . . . to borrow or lend abroad on long term on the average of the next few years'. Not only are such factors unfit for any quantitative representation, but it still remains unclear how they co-operate in the final result. In any case a calculation of the purchasing-power parities must be a preliminary and very important step in any endeavour to ascertain equilibrium rates of exchange. The said parities represent the first approximation to the rates we are trying to find. Other factors affecting these rates must be studied as causes of deviation from the purchasing-power parities. Anybody following the present international controversy over adequate exchange rates will find that an approximate calculation of purchasing-power parities always stands in the centre of the discussion. Thus actual practice follows the road indicated by theoretical analysis. It should also be observed, as I have pointed out elsewhere,[2] that 'other factors' have to

[1] *Money and Foreign Exchange after 1914*, pp. 137–62; *Theory of Social Economy*, 2nd ed., vol. ii, London 1932, pp. 513–16, 658–63.

[2] *Skand. Quarterly*, July 1934, and *Quantitative Thinking*, p. 46.

adjust themselves to the standard rates of exchange, when once such rates have been fixed; and that a stabilization is possible only when a fixation of exchanges has enforced such an adjustment.

Mr. Keynes thinks that an 'initial set of rates of exchange could be settled . . . by a process of trial and error'. 'As a test of success' he sets up 'the voluntary removal of all those exchange restrictions, import quotas, exceptional tariffs, &c., which are not desired for their own sake as a permanent feature of national policy'. The experimental period, according to Mr. Keynes, 'cannot even begin' until the gold countries have removed the existing disequilibrium of their exchanges, which he thinks practically possible only by revaluation of their currencies in terms of gold.

Thus the process of stabilization will after all be very much like that proposed by Sir Henry Strakosch: (1) an adjustment of internal price-levels in the several countries to a reasonable equilibrium between prices and cost; and (2) a fixing by international agreement, or at least in a spirit of mutual understanding, of exchange rates representing a reasonable equilibrium between the several currencies. Such an agreement, as Mr. Keynes rightly points out, cannot be reached 'if each Central Bank insists on being on the safe side . . . for what is the safe side for one bank is the unsafe side for all the others'. Assuming, however, that reasonable 'rates be discovered by impartial persons', and 'acceptable to the Central Banks', the world should have attained everything in the way of a stable monetary system that it can possibly hope to reach in any future that concerns us.

Mr. Keynes tacitly assumes—as is so commonly done—that such a system must be tied to gold. The question whether this is necessary or advisable is, however, a vital point which cannot simply be passed over. If the preceding survey of the downfall of the gold standard has proved anything, it is that the gold standard has lost all those qualities that once gave it a natural position as a basis of the world's monetary system. Private right to possess gold as money has already largely been suppressed and should, according to Mr. Keynes's proposals, be definitely abolished; private right to payment in gold or its equivalent has been suppressed just as radically as has been the security of redemption of notes in gold or of maintenance of fixed gold parities. The last remnant of confidence in the gold standard is destroyed when proposals for a restoration of such a standard are regularly accompanied by the reservation that the gold parities, at last established after many years of trial, must be regarded as provisional and subject to alterations so soon as these parities are felt to expose the various currencies to an undue stress. Mr. Keynes himself raises the question, 'Are we prepared to pledge ourselves in such circumstances to use all the other weapons open to us, however economically or politically injurious, rather than modify the gold-parity of our currency?' His answer is: 'Assuredly we are not.'

Under such circumstances it is really pertinent to ask, What in heaven's name is the sense of linking our currency system in any way to gold? The above inquiry has disclosed the serious dangers connected with a return to gold as a basis of our monetary system. The main consequences that we have to fear from such a backward step are: in the immediate future, an exaggerated rise in prices based on the superabundance of revalued gold reserves; later on, a new shortage of gold with a repetition of the deflation and the depression that we have just gone through; generally, we would have to reckon with a periodically recurrent aggravation of economic crises resulting from that competition for gold and that enhancement of its value which would always follow extraordinary endeavours to secure liquidity; further, the whole series of disturbances connected with the very controversial question of an equitable redistribution of the world's gold reserves and of the use to be made of these reserves for the supply of means of payment; not to speak of the perturbations that would follow if countries again began to accumulate disproportionate gold reserves; the general strengthening of protectionism throughout the world that always accompanies an acute international competition for gold; and finally, the constant presence of that element of insecurity which is instilled into economic life by the fear lest existing gold parities might again be abandoned.

In the report submitted by the Second Committee to the 1935 Assembly of the League of Nations[1] it is pointed out that 'the most gratifying and encouraging feature of the Second Committee's discussions consisted in the refusal of the different delegations to waste time on sterile debates on monetary policy. It was clear to them that, instead of debating theoretical points, it was better to try to find the elements of effective co-operation in the actual situation as it now stands. All the members of the Committee agreed that these elements existed and that such co-operation was possible.'

This seems to be a sensible and practical way of dealing with the monetary problem. Instead of drawing up more or less arbitrary programmes for the future we should devote ourselves to unbiased observation of the great process of recasting that the world's monetary system is actually going through. What in this process are the most positive and promising contributions to monetary reconstruction? The answer to this question can only be one. The

[1] Geneva, September 1935.

imperative need for a workable monetary organization has led to the establishment of a sterling bloc, which has now been at work practically for more than four years, and, in a more definite form, ever since the London Conference. This sterling bloc possesses a monetary system with very stable rates of exchange between the various currencies of the bloc, and with remarkable stability in the internal purchasing-power of those currencies.

The creation of this bloc proves that stabilization of exchanges is by no means such an insuperable and overwhelming task as it is often made out to be, or as it appears to be in Mr. Keynes's perspective of an 'experimental period' which would last 'long enough for the exchange rates to shake down to levels which can be maintained for the time being without excessive strain on any one'. Immediately after the London Conference Sweden fixed her rate of exchange on London at Kr. 19·40 and has since then maintained this rate practically invariable, Swedish prices and other economic factors being continually adjusted to it. This process has caused neither of the parties any undue strain; so far as can now be judged, Sweden's policy of joining the sterling bloc has been a great success—in spite of the singular difficulties obtaining. The same holds good with regard to Finland and Norway. Even Denmark, a country whose export trade has been most seriously impaired by foreign restrictions, has since the London Conference managed to keep her rate on London constant. The experience of British members of the sterling bloc points in the same direction. The objection should not be made that these examples refer only to small countries or to countries with a small population, and do not therefore afford any reliable evidence. Some of these countries have a rather specialized export trade, and big countries with a broader base for their international trade ought to experience less, and not greater, difficulties in maintaining a stable rate of exchange on London.

The continued adjustment of the economy of the sterling countries to the given currency system has doubtless the effect of increasing the internal strength of the sterling bloc. Confidence in this system has in fact grown year by year, and has certainly been one of the primary factors in the more and more manifest prosperity enjoyed by the sterling countries. The sterling bloc has also, as we have seen above, exerted a strong attraction, a number of other countries having joined the bloc, or at any rate approximately pegged their currencies to the pound, or else pursued a policy involving a certain *rapprochement* to the pound.

At present a further development of the sterling bloc stands out as the only hopeful line of progress. Perhaps one may find in addition some prospect of an approximate stabilization of the pound-dollar exchange, certainly not by formal agreement, but rather as a result of a natural balance between the efforts of the United States to raise, and those of England to lower, the rate. However, the American silver purchases on the world market have tended artificially to depreciate the dollar; and uncontrolled inflation still remains a serious threat to the internal stability of the dollar. Any American co-operation in the world's recovery necessarily presupposes that such extraordinary and unsound influences shall be eliminated.

This is all that can be said on the positive side of the present outlook. The other features of it are entirely negative. The value of gold itself is extremely unstable, and nobody can forecast its future. The gold bloc stands out more and more as an artificial and untenable construction. It is held together by rates of exchange incompatible with economic equilibrium, and its several price-levels are out of gear with costs of production and living—and still more so with the increasingly intolerable burden of public debts.

Still less can we discern any hope for the future in the various exchange-control systems to which a number of governments have resorted in emergency situations. In particular, the use in one and the same country of several parallel currencies with different legal status hardly opens up any very bright prospects for the future.

There remains the question whether the sterling bloc shall again be placed on a gold basis. It seems to be generally agreed by those who have given serious thought to this question that such a return can only be contemplated after the lapse of a long period of experimental approach to stabilization and after the fulfilment of certain essential conditions. Although views vary as to the procedure to be followed, and as to the nature of the conditions that must be fulfilled, it is hardly doubted that the restoration of the gold standard is the concern of a relatively distant future. Even the advocates of a provisional gold standard would not, on cross-examination, be able to defend a realization of their plans under present confused conditions.

Officially, of course, respectable people always have something to say about 'a future return to gold'. But this talk more and more assumes the character of a devotion to age-honoured ideals, nobody seriously considering a practical application of them. Leading authorities, when they speak of an ultimate return to gold, do not show much real faith in it. The remarkable speech which the Chancellor of the Exchequer delivered on the occasion of the Lord Mayor's Banquet at the Mansion House on 1 October 1935 is clear evidence of the extent to which recent experience has undermined the Chancellor's confidence in the gold standard. The following extract from his speech is well worth reproducing here:

'Of course all of us would like to get back as soon as possible to a stable common international monetary standard, which in practice means the gold standard. But I sometimes think that some of those who have been appealing for a British lead, those who dwell upon the advantage of having safe, stable currencies, do not always stop to consider the possible consequences of attempting to establish a rigid system in a world of instability, in a world where existing currencies are sadly out of equilibrium with one another, and where they cannot be adjusted without serious and perhaps dangerous political repercussions. After all, the essence of a stable monetary standard must be that the country which adheres to it must regulate its price level and its credit policies in respect of other important centres to which it is linked. Therefore if this country were to go back to a gold standard it would mean that we should no longer be free to adapt our policy in regard to price levels and cheap money to our own domestic requirements. We should have to adjust it according to conditions oversea over which we had no control, and at a time when international affairs are unsettled and when large movements of capital, quite sufficient to upset any newly established equilibrium, are by no means beyond the bounds of probability.

'Nor must we forget that in this matter we have not only our own interests to think of. A renewed fall in prices would be even more disastrous to the Dominions and to the Colonies than to ourselves, and I say they would have a just cause of grievance if we were to move without the utmost circumspection in a matter which so nearly concerns their vital interests.

'So it does not seem to me that the time has yet come when we can venture to tie our hands. We must wait a little longer with as much patience as we can muster until the international skies clear and until funds are more stable and the dollar and the franc can look one another in the face without a squint. In the meantime we are doing nothing to aggravate the situation, and I might even say we have done something to mitigate it. We have never tried to depreciate the pound, nor to snatch commercial advantage therefrom, and we never shall. We have never attempted to impose our monetary policy upon other people. We have contributed to the comparative stability of sterling throughout the sterling area, which in itself forms no small fraction of the surface of the globe. We have done something to bring back prosperity to our own country. So long as we freely buy the world's goods and freely pay for them, that is the best contribution that we can make to the prosperity of the world.'

The Hon. R. H. Brand, whose views on monetary matters always deserve the closest attention, reviews in the December (1935) issue of *Lloyds Bank Monthly* the discussion that has been going on in that journal ever since April. In giving his own opinions on the subject he displays an unmistakable sympathy for the gold standard. 'Gold', he writes, 'has one great merit, that politicians can do nothing with it; that it is something to which they must conform and that to break from it is a step which in ordinary circumstances they will be very reluctant to take.' Recent events have shown that this faith is no longer well founded. The up-to-date politician is not likely to be prevented by veneration for gold, or for any particular gold parity, from doing anything with his monetary system that he thinks to be in the interest of his country; and politicians in leading countries may very materially and in the most arbitrary way influence the value of gold. For the present, however, Mr. Brand rejects any idea of a restoration. He says: 'I am led to the opinion that we should put out of our minds for the present any thought of returning to the gold standard, in the sense of determining once and for all the parity of sterling with gold.'

How distant the realization of any programme for restoring the gold standard is will best be perceived if we consider the pre-conditions usually stated to be required for such a step. The probability of their fulfilment is very faint indeed. True, it may perhaps be assumed that the members of the gold bloc will devalue—or abandon—the gold standard within a relatively short time. But after such a step had been taken years would be required for an adjustment, both internal and external, to the new currency system. With regard to other conditions, such as the redistribution of gold reserves and the abolition of extraordinary restrictions on trade, exchange, and capital movements, it is hardly possible for anybody, in the present situation, to find grounds of hope for their fulfilment. In the last few months France has, it is true, exported large sums of gold; but this is more the result of severe political unrest and financial weakness than of a deliberate and well-considered monetary policy. The gold has gone to America, resulting in a still worse maldistribution of the world's monetary gold stock. Again, as to freedom of trade, there has certainly been no lack of fine declarations, but these are usually made conditional upon such monetary measures as are most unlikely to be carried out. Recent utterances of liberal members of the American Government are no doubt very sound and very remarkable in the sympathy expressed for an unhampered import of goods; and the bilateral foreign trade agreements recently concluded by the United States should open up good prospects for a more unrestricted international exchange of goods; but the value of this policy depends entirely upon the very uncertain future of the American currency.

Turning now to gold itself, everybody must admit that there is nothing in the present situation that indicates the beginning of a stabilization of its value. The enormous increase in the production of gold that has taken place in recent years as a result of extraordinary circumstances certainly cannot be regarded as a guarantee of stability in the value of that metal. Gold movements are more arbitrary and more violent than ever, and great and unforeseeable variations in the value of gold may take place. The means for controlling such variations, which theoretically have been made clear enough, are now farther away than ever from practical application. It can hardly be otherwise so long as the demand for gold reserves is steadily increasing on the neo-mercantilistic assumption that they form the essence of the wealth of nations and an indispensable basis of political and military power. The present concentration of gold in the United States is a particularly disquieting development. The appalling sway that dilettante money-panaceas exert over the public mind in that country may produce incalculable effects, from which the value of gold can certainly not be isolated. America has won a dominating influence on the gold market; yet the balance of power in that country is anything but reassuring for the use of that influence.

In this situation there seems to be very little sense in holding out the prospect of a return to gold as a standard for our monetary units. Nobody really believes in such a restoration, nobody has any confidence in its tenability. The numerous proposals for some provisional adoption of the gold standard have only contributed to increase the distrust in this system. The public will never believe that a restored gold standard will be anything but provisional. On the other hand, the dangers of again linking our currencies to gold are beginning to be more and more clearly perceived. The present book has demonstrated the deep reality of these dangers.

If gold cannot be restored to its old place as the basis of the world's monetary system, this does not necessarily mean that we must entirely dispense with the services of gold for monetary purposes. It would be unwise to make any abrupt changes in the present custom of keeping gold as a reserve or as a means for international settlements. Only, our monetary standard and the supply of means of payment valid in that standard must be kept entirely independent of gold. How the demand for gold will develop under such conditions we cannot foretell. It may be found possible to avoid serious disturbances of the market for gold. But this problem must henceforth be regarded as separate from and altogether subordinate to the great task of providing the world with a stable monetary system.

To summarize our conclusions: A restoration of the gold standard is not to be reckoned with. The belief in the gold standard may still live on for some years as a creed to which people pay lip-service. But for all practical purposes the gold standard is a thing that belongs to the past. We are actually passing through a period of transformation in which the foundations of a new and more reliable monetary system are being laid. This task is the concern of those who have their eyes turned towards the future. What has happened since 1928, when the first tentative restoration of the gold standard was accomplished, has fully justified the title of this work: the Downfall of the Gold Standard now stands out as the most prominent and definite feature of the economic history of our generation.

INDEX

Abyssinia, 194.
Acts, American, 117–21, 125, 133, 171, 179, 181, 185.
British, 39, 42, 64.
Appreciation, 107, 239.
Approximation, 243.
Argentine, 61, 204.
Australia, 61, 94, 170.
Austria, 215.
Avenol, 27.

Bank for International Settlements, 150, 185–6, 206, 231.
(Other banks, *see* countries.)
Belgium, 60, 155, 191–4, 209, 241.
Bianchini, 27.
Bimetallism, 160, 162, 171, 176–7, 182.
Blackett, 27, 89, 210.
Bonnet, 202.
Boom, 12, 89, 222, 228–9.
Boothby, 90.
Brand, 27, 254.
Brazil, 61.
British Dominions, 42, 155–6, 252.
Brownell, 178–9.
Bruce, 94–5.

Canada, 61, 170.
Capital movements (transfers), 3, 49–52, 59, 131, 215, 220, 226, 252, 255.
Capitalism, 69–71.
Carnegie Endowment, 231.
Cassel, 21, 24–5, 27, 30, 33–4, 66, 81–2, 85–7, 116, 144–5, 148.
Chamberlain, 96, 134, 141, 186.
Chancellor of the Exchequer, 36, 92, 95–6, 141, 150, 155–6, 210, 251.
Chile, 61.
China, 11, 110, 159, 162, 165, 168, 170, 174–8, 204.
China Association, 166.
Churchill, 36, 39–42, 44, 91.
Coin, 23, 30, 41–2, 54, 110, 120, 124, 128, 200.
Collijn, 101, 196.
Commissions, Indian Currency and Finance, 42.
Preparatory, *see* League of Nations.
Committees, Genoa, of Experts, 27, 31.
Economists' National, 234.
Further, *see* League of Nations.
Conferences, Antwerp, 238.
Basle, 100.
Brussels, 21, 25, 56.
Geneva, 52.
Genoa, § 5, 34, 36, 41, 46, 56.
Lausanne, 101, 105–6, 113–14, 135.
London, 98, 102, 106, 109, Ch. VI, 170, 184, 199, 210, 240, 242.
Ottawa, 86, 94, 97–8.

Congress (U.S.A.), 117, 122–3, 131, 169, 181, 185.
Cost of living, 250.
of production, 142, 205, 235, 242, 244, 250.
Cover, 17, 110, 160, 213, 218, 223.
Credit, 12, 30, 61, 113, 139, 143, 183, 197, 206, 218, 252.
Crises, 18, 246.
Crisis, 1907, 14.
1929, 36, 62–3.
1929–35, § 11, 100, 102, 114, 130, 159, 201.
Currencies, *see* countries.
Czechoslovakia, 191, 209.

Dawes, 35.
Denmark, 248.
Depreciation, 107, 136, 148, 183, 186, 199, 206, 228, 239, 250.
Desborough, 167.
Deterding, 167–8.
Devaluation, 33, 192–3, 197, 209, 228, 236–7, 241.
Discount policy, 13.
Dubois, 27, 30.

Elliot, 90–1.
Empire Declaration, 157.
Encyclopaedia Britannica, 229.
England, *see* Great Britain.
Excess reserves, 18, 187, 219–22.
Exchange, Equalization Fund (Account), 89, 90, 93–4, 156, 182, 185–6.
on London, 5, 240, 248–9.
pound-dollar rate, 186, 250.

Federal Reserve System (banks), 63, 118–22.
Finland, 248.
Fisher, 61.
France, 32, § 8, 59–61, 68, 73, 100, 107, 139, 149, 155, 189, 194, 196–203, 208, 217, 221, 231, 237, 241, 255.

Germany, 35, 100, 215.
Gold, bloc, 155–6, § 26, 250, 254.
centres, 29, 30.
clause, 122.
distribution, 2, 4, 53.
economizing policy, 10, 30, 41–2, 79, 82, 110, 161.
international movements, 3, 13.
maldistribution, 53.
mentality, 67, 107.
monetary stock, 8.
production, 9, 54, 227, 229, 255.
purchasing-power, 55–6, 72.
scarcity, 10, 11, 67, 200, 219, 229.
shortness (shortage), 53–4, 60, 131, 161, 227, 246.
supply, 7.
total stock, 8.
value, 5, § 2, 24–5, 41, 45, 51, 65, 67–8, 75, 79, 82, 84, 200, 203, 229–30, 232–3, 241, 246, 255–6.
Gold Delegation, *see* League of Nations.
Gold reserve, 17.
as basis for payments, § 28.
as regulator of credit, § 29.

Gold reserve, (*cont.*)
immobilized, 18.
legal minimum, 18, 161.
Gold-standard system, international, Ch. I, 45–7, 50, 52, 226.
post-War reconstruction, 1, Ch. II, 258.
Governor of Bank of England, 150.
Great Britain (England), § 6, § 7, 48, 64–7, 83, § 13, 114, 135–6, 149, 169, 194, 199, 205–8, 210, 231, 250.
Greenway, 167.

Harrod, 238.
Havenstein, 17, 27.
Henderson, 238.
Herriot, 139.
Hoarding (hoards), 13, 50, 120, 122, 128, 227–8, 237, 241.
Holland (Netherlands), 42, 60, 155, 194, 196, 221, 233.
Hoover, 100, 112, 114–15.
Horne, 91, 166.
Hunsdon, 167.

India, 42, 94, 162, 165, 170, 178, 228.
International Chamber of Commerce, 232.
Italy, 140, 151, 194, 215, 241.

Jansen, 74.
Japan, 175, 204, 225.
Justice, 78.

Keynes, 37, 99, 238, 241–5.

Laval, 197–8.
Lawrie, 173, 184.
Layton, 101.
League of Nations, 56–7, 102.
Assembly, 116, 233, 247.
Council, 56.
Economic Committee, 116, 234.
Financial Committee, 55, 58.
Gold Delegation, 57–8, 72–6, 80–2, 107, 150, 161, 219.
Preparatory Commission, § 15, 135–8, 144–5, 150.
Second Committee, 233, 247.
Survey, 195–6, 206, 227–8.
Leith Ross, 175.
Liquidity, 63, 130, 215, 246.
Loucheur, 53.
Luther, 35.

Mabane, 90.
MacDonald, 137.
Maladjustment, 62, 71, 74–5.
Maldistribution, 220, 226, 255.
Managed Currency, 2, 3.
Mant, 74.
Mexico, 160, 170, 176–7.
Mooly, 153.
Morgenthau, 176.

Nanking Government, 175–6.
New Zealand, 61.
Norway, 248.
Notes, 17, 18.

Ohlin, 238.
Oriental Economist, 225.
Overproduction, 62–3.
Overvaluation, 169, 174, 178, 191, 195–6, 201.

Paraguay, 61.
Peru, 61, 170.
Pitman, 170.
Poincaré, 47, 53.
Poland, 155, 194–5.
Power, 87, 99, 210, 256.
Progress, 8, 10, 43, 77.
Protectionism, 14, 25, 49, 53, 70–1, 114, 226, 247.
Purchasing-power parity, 48, 240–3.

Quotas, 138, 199, 244.

Redemption (Redeemability), § 3, 65, 129.
Reparations, 12, 23–6, 49, 53, 57, 70–1, 82, 96, § 14, 113.
Right, individual (private), 19, 128–31, 245.
Roosevelt, 116, 133, 136, 151, 153, 171, 185, 188, 222, 226.
Russia, 26, 27.
Rydbeck, 101.

Salter, 239.
Sauerbeck, 7.
Schacht, 35, 214.
Schuster, 94.
Silver, 110–11, Ch. VII, 182–3, 190, 221, 250.
Silver Association, 167.
Snowden, 39–41, 64–5.
Socialism, 69, 71.
Spain, 170.
Statist, The, 162, 164.
Sterling: Bloc (Group), 4, 83–8, 97–8, 157–8, 174, 193–4, 201–2, § 27, 235, 248, 251.
standard, 16, § 13.
Strakosch, 27, 72, 74, 235–8, 242, 244.
Sweden, 35–8, 65–6, 144, 208, 218, 248.
Switzerland, 42, 60, 155, 194–5, 221.

Teunis, 192.
Thomas Amendment, 120–1.
Times, The, 153–6.
Trade Union, 38, 68.
Trip, 196.

Undervaluation, 48–9, 104, 109–10, 148, 168, 183, 186, 193.
Unemployment, 103, 228.
United States (America), 11, 14, 37, 41, 45, 59–63, 73, 88, 112, 114–15, §§ 17–19, 144–5, 149, 151–2, §§ 23–5, 217–22, 231, 234, 237, 250, 255–6.
Uruguay, 61.

Venezuela, 61.
Vissering, 27.

War debts, 12, 23, 25, 53, 83, 96, 99, 101, 114–15, 135.
Wealth of Nations, 256.
Webb, 167.

van Zeeland, 192.